Latin
FOR COMMON ENTRANCE

13+
LEVEL 2

Exam
Practice
Answers

R.C. Bass

GALORE
PARK

AN HACHETTE UK COMPANY

About the author

Bob Bass taught at prep schools in Somerset, Kenya and Sussex before moving in 1987 to Orwell Park, Ipswich, where he is Head of Classics and Senior Master. He has served on the editorial board of the *Journal of Classics Teaching* and on the Council of the Joint Association of Classical Teachers. For 12 years he edited the SATIPS Classics Broadsheet, and has been IAPS' Subject Leader and then Subject Adviser in Classics. He is the Chief Setter of ISEB's Common Entrance and Common Academic Scholarship Latin papers, proof-reader for their Greek papers, and an IGCSE examiner. He is the author of various Latin and Greek resources targeted at young learners.

Every effort has been made to trace all copyright holders, but if any have been inadvertently overlooked, the Publishers will be pleased to make the necessary arrangements at the first opportunity.

Although every effort has been made to ensure that website addresses are correct at time of going to press, Galore Park cannot be held responsible for the content of any website mentioned in this book. It is sometimes possible to find a relocated web page by typing in the address of the home page for a website in the URL window of your browser.

Hachette UK's policy is to use papers that are natural, renewable and recyclable products and made from wood grown in sustainable forests. The logging and manufacturing processes are expected to conform to the environmental regulations of the country of origin.

Orders: please contact Bookpoint Ltd, 130 Milton Park, Abingdon, Oxon OX14 4SB. Telephone: (44) 01235 827720. Fax: (44) 01235 400454. Email education@bookpoint.co.uk Lines are open from 9 a.m. to 5 p.m., Monday to Saturday, with a 24-hour message answering service. Visit our website at www.galorepark.co.uk for details of other revision guides for Common Entrance, examination papers and Galore Park publications.

ISBN: 978 1 471853 48 7

© Robert C. Bass 2015

First published in 2015 by
Galore Park Publishing Ltd,
An Hachette UK Company
Carmelite House
50 Victoria Embankment
London EC4Y 0DZ

www.galorepark.co.uk

Impression number   10 9 8 7 6 5 4 3 2 1

Year   2019 2018 2017 2016 2015

Typeset in India

Printed in the United Kingdom

A catalogue record for this title is available from the British Library.

Contents

Introduction

A note on translation into English

The present tense in Latin may be translated using either of two aspects: the present simple (**amo** = I love) or the present continuous/progressive (**amo** = I am loving).

The imperfect tense may be translated as either **amabam** = I was loving or **amabam** = I used to love.

The perfect tense may be translated as a simple past (**amavi** = I loved) or as a 'true' perfect (**amavi** = I have loved).

Note also that, as Latin has neither a definite article nor an indefinite article, the use of 'the' and 'a/an' can often be interchangeable. Pupils should not, as this stage, be penalised where their choice does not match the answers given here.

Equally, the 3rd person singular may be translated by 'he', 'she' or 'it'. Again, pupils should not be penalised where their choice does not match the answers given.

This answer book tends to use whichever makes the most sense in the context of the piece. Pupils should not (at this stage) be penalised for using a form that, while grammatically correct, is not given as the example answer in this book.

The syllabus and your exams

For Common Entrance Latin, you will sit an exam lasting one hour. You will choose one of the three levels, Level 1, Level 2 or Level 3, as agreed with your teacher.

The format of each level is the same, but the material gets harder. In each level, there are four questions worth a total of 75 marks, as follows:

Question 1 (15 marks)

A short passage of Latin will be set, on which you will be asked to answer eight to ten questions, testing your understanding of the passage. You will not be expected to write a translation of the passage, but clearly you need to have translated it in your head, in order to answer the questions.

Question 2 (30 marks)

Another, slightly longer passage will be set, continuing the story from the passage in Question 1. You will be asked to translate this passage, writing your translation on alternate lines.

Question 3 (20 marks)

Another short passage of Latin will be set, continuing the story from the earlier two passages. Questions will be set, testing your knowledge of Latin grammar and how the language works. You will not be asked to translate this passage, but again you will find it difficult to answer the questions unless you have translated it for yourself.

The questions will fall into the following types:

- From the passage give, in Latin, one example of: (an adjective, a preposition followed by the accusative, a noun in the genitive, a verb in the imperfect tense, etc.)

- **erat** (line 2). In which tense is this verb? What is the 1st person singular of the present tense of this verb?

- **pueros** (line 4). In which case is this noun? Why is this case used?

- **vocaverunt** (line 5). What does this word mean? What is the connection between **vocaverunt** and the English word *vocation*?

- **necat** (line 5) means *he kills*. How would you say in Latin *he was killing* (imperfect tense)?

  And last but not least:

- Using the vocabulary given, translate the following two short sentences into Latin.

Most candidates lose the majority of their marks on Question 3 by falling into the trap of thinking they do not need to translate the passage. They simply guess the answers. To answer a question such as 'in which case is the word **templum** in line 3?', you have to have translated the sentence in which the word **templum** is. Otherwise you will simply be guessing, particularly with a word such as **templum**, which could be any of nominative, vocative or accusative singular.

Question 4 (10 marks)

You will be set eight questions on four areas: Roman domestic life; the city of Rome; the army and Roman Britain; and Greek mythology. Each question will have two parts, part (i) and part (ii). You select **one** question, and answer both parts of it. Examples are given below:

The city of Rome

(c) (i) Tell the story of Cloelia.

   (ii) Which elements of this story would the Romans have found particularly admirable? Explain your answer.

Greek mythology

(h) (i) Tell the story of Odysseus' encounter with the Cyclops.

   (ii) Describe two qualities which Odysseus displayed in this encounter.

These are two of the eight questions that might have been set, labelled (a) to (h). If you had chosen to do the one labelled (c) above, you would have done both part (i) and part (ii) of that question.

Tips on revising

Get the best out of your brain

- Give your brain plenty of oxygen by exercising. You can only revise effectively if you feel fit and well.

- Eat healthy food while you are revising. Your brain works better when you give it good fuel.

- Think positively. Give your brain positive messages so that it will want to study.

- Keep calm. If your brain is stressed, it will not operate effectively.

- Take regular breaks during your study time.

- Get enough sleep. Your brain will carry on sorting out what you have revised while you sleep.

Get the most from your revision

- Don't work for hours without a break. Revise for 20–30 minutes, then take a five-minute break.

- Do good things in your breaks: listen to your favourite music, eat healthy food, drink some water, do some exercise or juggle. Don't read a book, watch TV or play on the computer; it will conflict with what your brain is trying to learn.

- When you go back to your revision, review what you have just learnt.

- Regularly review the material you have learnt.

Get motivated

- Set yourself some goals and promise yourself a treat when the exams are over.

- Make the most of all the expertise and talent available to you at school and at home. If you don't understand something, ask your teacher to explain.

- Get organised. Find a quiet place to revise and make sure you have all the equipment you need.

- Use year and weekly planners to help you organise your time so that you revise all subjects equally. (Available for download from www.galorepark.co.uk)

- Use topic and subject checklists to help you keep on top of what you are revising. (Available for download from www.galorepark.co.uk)

Know what to expect in the exam

- Use past papers to familiarise yourself with the format of the exam.

- Make sure you understand the language examiners use.

Before the exam

- Have all your equipment and pens ready the night before.

- Make sure you are at your best by getting a good night's sleep before the exam.

- Have a good breakfast in the morning.

- Take some water into the exam if you are allowed.

- Think positively and keep calm.

During the exam

- Have a watch on your desk. Work out how much time you need to allocate to each question and try to stick to it.

- Make sure you read and understand the instructions on the front of the exam paper.

- Allow some time at the start to read and consider the questions carefully before writing anything.

- Read every question at least twice. Don't rush into answering before you have a chance to think about it.

Exercise 1.1

1 You were.

2 They loved.

3 They run.

4 We see.

5 You were writing.

6 I fight.

7 He answers.

8 He answered.

9 We were staying.

10 They shout.

1 mark for each question. Total: 10

Exercise 1.2

1 You lead.

2 You say.

3 They played.

4 We send.

5 We moved.

6 You departed.

7 You were attacking.

8 You show.

9 He prepared.

10 I put.

1 mark for each question. Total: 10

Exercise 1.3

1 We see.

2 They overcame.

3 You were.

4 You were carrying.

5 They hear.

6 He killed.

7 They kill.

8 He moved.

9 He ordered.

10 He gives.

1 mark for each question. Total: 10

Exercise 1.4

1 They decided.

2 He took.

3 I wanted.

4 He was leading.

5 We threw.

6 You praise.

7 They stood.

8 You carried.

9 You send.

10 We were hurrying.

1 mark for each question. Total: 10

Exercise 1.5

1 We were running quickly.

2 He was fighting bravely.

3 They sailed for a long time.

4 I never play.

5 You write well.

6 They often used to cry.

7 I slept for a long time.

8 They finally departed.

9 He suddenly entered.

10 He is always drinking.

2 marks for each question. Total: 20

Exercise 1.6

1 The Romans built a big town. (4)

2 The sailor was not afraid of the dangers. (4)

3 A crowd of women was standing in the street. (5)

4 You said many words. (3)

5 The Romans destroyed many temples. (4)

Total: 20

Exercise 1.7

1 The new town has high walls. (5)

2 Many sailors are approaching quickly. (4)

3 Today I am working. Yesterday however I did nothing. (6)

4 The Romans were carrying many shields. (4)

5 Many good men fought in the battle. (6)

Total: 25

Exercise 1.8

1 The messengers hurried into the sacred temple.

2 Once many Romans were famous.

3 The wicked master killed the miserable slave.

4 The beautiful maidservants were preparing good food.

5 Bad boys never listen to teachers.

5 marks for each question. Total: 25

Exercise 1.9

1 The teacher frightened the boy with angry words.

2 We always fight with swords and shields.

3 The master gave much money to the slave.

4 I killed the small boy with my spear.

5 The famous poet was reading a good book.

5 marks for each question. Total: 25

Exercise 1.10

1 The words of the sailors were bad. (4)

2 Crowds of slaves are coming. (3)

3 The walls of the temple are high and strong. (6)

4 The friend of the boy was singing. (3)

5 We never listen to the words of the teacher. (4)

Total: 20

Exercise 1.11

1 They love to play. (2)

2 The slave wanted to fight. (3)

3 The master ordered the slave to work. (4)

4 I never want to work. (3)

5 The messenger decides/decided to run. (3)

Total: 15

Exercise 1.12

1 Walk slowly, boys!

2 Write a book, poet!

3 Move the horses, farmers!

4 Drink wine, friend!

5 Abandon your weapons, sailors!

3 marks for each question. Total: 15

Exercise 1.13

1 The boy was standing in the road.

2 The slaves fought against the master.

3 We are in great danger.

4 The messenger ran along the street.

5 The girl is playing with her friends.

4 marks for each question. Total: 20

1 Was the farmer looking at the sky for a long time? (4)

2 Did the teacher say bad words? (4)

3 Are the slaves attacking the wall? (3)

4 Do the boys have shields? (3)

5 Did the master have many slaves and maidservants? (6)

Total: 20

Exercise 1.15

1 They laugh.	3rd person	Plural	Present	rideo
2 He was attacking.	3rd person	Singular	Imperfect	oppugno
3 We were putting.	1st person	Plural	Imperfect	pono
4 You gave.	2nd person	Plural	Perfect	do
5 They stood.	3rd person	Plural	Perfect	sto
6 They worked.	3rd person	Plural	Perfect	laboro
7 They decide.	3rd person	Plural	Present	constituo
8 You ran.	2nd person	Plural	Perfect	curro
9 They wrote.	3rd person	Plural	Perfect	scribo
10 We were preparing.	1st person	Plural	Imperfect	paro

5 marks for each question. Total: 50

Exercise 1.16

1 They come.	3rd person	Plural	Present	venio
2 He was.	3rd person	Singular	Imperfect	sum
3 You were carrying.	2nd person	Singular	Imperfect	porto
4 You kill.	2nd person	Singular	Present	neco
5 They drank.	3rd person	Plural	Perfect	bibo
6 You were sleeping.	2nd person	Singular	Imperfect	dormio
7 He ordered.	3rd person	Singular	Perfect	iubeo
8 He warns.	3rd person	Singular	Present	moneo
9 You took.	2nd person	Singular	Perfect	capio
10 They were saying.	3rd person	Plural	Imperfect	dico

5 marks for each question. Total: 50

Exercise 1.17

1 amabam.   I was loving.

2 estis.   You are.

3 cucurristi.   You ran.

4 posuerunt.   They put.

5 dormiebamus.   We were sleeping.

2 marks for each question. Total: 10

Exercise 1.18

1 videt.   He sees.

2 bibebatis.   You were drinking.

3 diximus.   We said.

4 festinant.   They hurry.

5 monuisti.   You warned.

2 marks for each question. Total: 10

Exercise 1.19

1 fuit.   He was.

2 tenebam.   I was holding.

3 regis.   You rule.

4 ridet.   He laughs.

5 faciebas.   You were doing.

2 marks for each question. Total: 10

Exercise 1.20

1 oppida oppugnamus.   We are attacking the town.

2 equos habebatis.   You used to have horses.

3 puellas spectaverunt.   They looked at the girls.

4 pericula timent.   They fear the dangers.

5 terras regebant.   They were ruling the lands.

2 + 2 marks for each question. Total: 20

Exercise 1.21

1 puellae pueros amant.   Girls like boys.

2 magistri libros iaciunt.   The teachers are throwing books.

3 pueri scuta habent.

The boys have shields.

4 ancillae cibos parant.

The maidservants are preparing foods.

5 nautae muros aedificant.

The sailors are building walls.

3 + 3 marks for each question. Total: 30

Exercise 1.22

1 agricolae hastas portabant.

The farmers were carrying spears.

2 viri pericula timebant.

The men were afraid of the dangers.

3 domini servos puniverunt.

The masters punished the slaves.

4 pueri magistros audiverunt.

The boys listened to the teachers.

5 poetae libros scripserunt.

The poets wrote books.

3 + 3 marks for each question. Total: 30

Exercise 1.23

1 ancillam habebam.

I used to have a maidservant.

2 gladium portas.

You are carrying a sword.

3 deam vidit.

He saw the goddess.

4 periculum timebas.

You were afraid of the danger.

5 virum laudavi.

I praised the man.

2 + 2 marks for each question. Total: 20

Exercise 1.24

1 servus templum aedificavit.

The slave built the temple.

2 nauta scutum portabat.

The sailor was carrying a shield.

3 puer malus erat.

The boy was bad.

4 regina terram regit.

The queen rules the land.

5 servus dominum necavit.

The slave killed the master.

3 + 3 marks for each question. Total: 30

Exercise 1.25

1 nauta feminam non timebat.

The sailor was not afraid of the woman.

2 agricola agrum amat.

The farmer likes the field.

3 oppidum murum habebat.

The town had a wall.

4 magister puerum puniebat.

The teacher was punishing the boy.

5 puella deum laudabat.

The girl was praising the god.

3 + 3 marks for each question. Total: 30

Exercise 2.1

Once upon a time the gods and goddesses were holding a celebration on Mount Olympus.[8] They were eating food and drinking wine.[5] They were holding a celebration because Peleus was marrying Thetis.[5] Thetis was a goddess.[3] Peleus was a mortal man.[4] The gods and goddesses were happy.[5] They were laughing.[1] Suddenly however Discord, a wicked goddess, entered.[6] When the rest of the gods saw Discord,[5] they were not happy.[3] They were not laughing now.[3] They were not laughing because they did not like Discord.[6] They shouted: 'What do you want, Discord?[4] Why are you standing here? [3] We don't like you.[3] Leave immediately!'[2] Discord announced:[2] 'Listen to me, gods![3] Listen to me, goddesses![3] I have a gift.[2] I have a beautiful gift.[3] Here it is.'[2] Then Discord put down an apple.[4] She laughed and departed.[3] The gods and goddesses approached the apple.[5] They looked at the apple.[2]

Total: 95

Exercise 2.2

1 (a) celebrabant/consumebant/bibebant/ducebat/erat/erant/ridebant/amabant. (1)

  (b) intravit/viderunt/clamaverunt/nuntiavit/deposuit/risit/
     discessit/appropinquaverunt/spectaverunt. (1)

  (c) erat/erant/est. (1)

  (d) discede/audite. (1)

  (e) te/me. (1)

2 Vocative. (1)

3 3rd person   Singular   Perfect   **rideo** (4)

Total: 10

Exercise 2.3

1 (a) pueri semper currunt clamantque. (1)

  (b) The boys are always running and shouting. (5)

2 (a) Iulia Valeriaque sunt puellae. (1)

  (b) Julia and Valeria are girls. (5)

3 (a) agricolae nautaeque veniunt. (1)

  (b) The farmers and sailors are coming. (4)

4 (a) currimus ludimusque. (1)

  (b) We are running and playing. (3)

5 (a) amici rident luduntque. (1)

  (b) The friends are laughing and playing. (4)

6 (a) servus est fessus laetusque. (1)

  (b) The slave is tired and happy. (5)

7 (a) puer cibum aquamque habet. (1)

  (b) The boy has food and water. (5)

8 (a) contra Romanos Graecosque pugnamus. (1)

  (b) We are fighting against the Romans and Greeks. (5)

9 (a) agricolae hastas sagittasque habent. (1)

  (b) The farmers have spears and arrows. (5)

10 (a) pueri intrant laborantque. (1)

  (b) The boys enter and work. (4)

Total: 55

Exercise 2.4

1 Marcus and Sextus are boys. (5)

2 I am laughing and playing. (3)

3 The boy and girl are running. (4)

4 The slave is afraid and flees. (4)

5 The boys run and play. (4)

6 The slaves and masters are coming. (4)

7 The teacher warns the boys and girls. (5)

8 The master enters and punishes the slave. (5)

9 The girl enters and sees a friend. (5)

10 The boys and girls laugh and play. (6)

Total: 45

Exercise 2.5

1 Romulus and Remus were Romans. (5)

2 We are always laughing and playing. (4)

3 Valeria and Aurelia are Roman girls. (6)

4 The teacher punishes Sextus and Marcus. (5)

5 Sextus and Marcus listen to the teacher. (5)

6 The teacher was looking at the boy and girl. (5)

7 The boy was afraid of the farmers and sailors. (5)

8 The slaves had food and water. (5)

9 The slaves were tired and miserable. (5)

10 The temple was sacred and beautiful. (5)

Total: 50

Exercise 2.6

1 You frightened.

2 They asked.

3 They destroyed.

4 We sent.

5 He saw.

6 You heard.

7 They decided.

8 You shouted.

9 We ruled.

10 He comes/He came.

1 mark for each question. Total: 10

Exercise 2.7

1 He said.

2 He ordered.

3 We ran.

4 He announced.

5 You made.

6 We stayed

7 You took.

8 They approached.

9 I drank.

10 He was.

1 mark for each question. Total: 10

Exercise 2.8

1 timui.

2 amavimus.

3 fuerunt.

4 vidisti.

5 dedistis.

6 audivit.

7 duximus.

8 risit.

9 rexi.

10 steterunt.

1 mark for each question. Total: 10

Exercise 2.9

1 movimus.

2 nuntiavi.

3 posuistis.

4 fuimus.

5 constituit.

6 cepi.

7 scripsisti.

8 iecerunt.

9 appropinquavimus.

10 discesserunt.

1 mark for each question. Total: 10

Exercise 2.10

1 appropinquabamus.	We were approaching.	(1 + 1)
2 discipuli laborant.	The pupils are working.	(2 + 2)
3 servi pugnabant.	The slaves were fighting.	(2 + 2)
4 pueri boni sunt.	The boys are good.	(3 + 3)
5 nautae navigaverunt.	The sailors sailed.	(2 + 2)

Total: 20

Exercise 2.11

1 liber bonus est.	The book is good.	(3 + 3)
2 gladium portabas.	You were carrying a sword.	(2 + 2)
3 bellum timeo.	I am afraid of the war.	(2 + 2)
4 nauta magnam hastam iecit.	The sailor threw a big spear.	(3 + 3)
5 servus murum altum aedificabat.	The slave was building a high wall.	(4 + 4)

Total: 30

Exercise 2.12

1 nuntiabam.	I was announcing.
2 navigavistis.	You sailed.
3 aedificat.	He builds.
4 steti.	I stood.
5 fuerunt.	They were/They have been.

2 marks for each question. Total: 10

Exercise 2.13

1 puella non cantat.	The girl is not singing.	(2 + 3)
2 donum pulchrum est.	The gift is beautiful.	(3 + 3)
3 servus murum aedificabat.	The slave was building a wall.	(3 + 3)
4 puer scutum portavit.	The boy carried a shield.	(3 + 3)
5 discipulus magistrum saepe timet.	The pupil often fears the teacher.	(3 + 4)

Total: 30

Exercise 2.14

1 He announced.	3rd	Singular	Perfect	nuntio
2 They were approaching.	3rd	Plural	Imperfect	appropinquo
3 You threw.	2nd	Singular	Perfect	iacio
4 We attack.	1st	Plural	Present	oppugno
5 He ordered.	3rd	Singular	Perfect	iubeo

5 marks for each question. Total: 25

Exercise 2.15

1 appropinquabant.	They were approaching.
2 nuntiabat.	He was announcing.
3 navigabam.	I was sailing.
4 oppugnabas.	You were attacking.
5 iubebat.	He was ordering.
6 iubebant.	They were ordering.
7 superabamus.	We were overcoming.
8 stabat.	He was standing.
9 delebant.	They were destroying.
10 dabamus.	We were giving.

2 marks for each question. Total: 20

Exercise 3.1

The gods and goddesses were on Mount Olympus.[7] They were looking at the apple.[2] The apple was beautiful.[3] The apple was golden.[3] These words were on the apple:[5] 'This golden apple is for the most beautiful woman.'[6] Juno was the queen of the gods.[4] She was both the sister and wife of Jupiter.[6] The goddess Juno looked at the apple.[4] She read the words.[2] 'I am the most beautiful goddess,' she shouted.[4] 'The apple is therefore mine.'[4] The goddess Athena looked at the apple.[4] She read the words.[2] 'You are wrong, Juno,' she shouted.[3] 'The apple is mine.[3] The apple is mine because I am the most beautiful.'[7] The goddess Venus looked at the apple.[4] She read the words. [2] 'You are wrong, goddesses.[2] I am the most beautiful.[2] The apple is therefore mine.[4] Hand over the apple to me!'[3] In this way the three goddesses were arguing about the golden apple.[7] They all wanted to have the golden apple.[5] They therefore decided to approach Jupiter.[5] Jupiter was both the father and king of the gods.[7]

Total: 110

Exercise 3.2

1 (a) tradite (1)

  (b) habere/appropinquare (1)

2 Ablative. After the preposition in, meaning 'on'. (2)

3 Genitive. Masculine. (2)

4 3rd person   Singular   Imperfect   sum (4)

Total: 10

Exercise 3.3

1 patres.

2 uxoris.

3 montibus.

4 matre.

5 sororum.

6 patri.

7 uxoribus.

8 sororem.

9 patres.

10 rex.

1 mark for each question. Total: 10

Exercise 3.4

1 regis.
2 uxor.
3 matri.
4 pater.
5 fratribus.

6 montem.
7 sorore.
8 matres.
9 fratribus.
10 patrum.

1 mark for each question. Total: 10

Exercise 3.5

1 montes.
2 patri.
3 rex!
4 uxores.
5 fratrem.

6 sororis.
7 patribus.
8 montis.
9 regi.
10 regum.

1 mark for each question. Total: 10

Exercise 3.6

1 montibus.
2 sorori.
3 fratres!
4 uxorum.
5 uxori.

6 sororem.
7 matres.
8 patribus.
9 fratribus.
10 matres.

1 mark for each question. Total: 10

Exercise 3.7

1 I saw the mountain. (2)
2 Father is running. (2)
3 I love my wife. (3)
4 The king rules. (2)
5 We love mother. (2)
6 I have a brother and sister. (4)
7 The king has a beautiful sister. (4)
8 We saw many mountains. (3)

9 We were approaching the high mountain. (4)

10 My wife is now coming/has already come. (4)

Total: 30

Exercise 3.8

1 Marcus is the brother of Aurelia. (4)

2 Aurelia is the sister of Marcus. (4)

3 The girl was preparing food for her father. (4)

4 The girl does not like her sister. (4)

5 The slaves are hurrying towards the mountain. (4)

6 In the mountains there are many roads. (5)

7 The king loved his mother and father. (4)

8 The king had a beautiful wife. (4)

9 I have a good father. (3)

10 My sister is bad. (4)

Total: 40

Exercise 3.9

1 The boy is always fighting with his sister. (5)

2 The girl is always fighting with her brother. (5)

3 The father of the boy is angry. (4)

4 The king rules the land well. (4)

5 The king gives money to his sister. (4)

6 The girl takes the king's money. (4)

7 My mother has a famous brother. (5)

8 The brother of my mother was famous. (5)

9 The boy gave many gifts to his mother. (5)

10 The wife of the king is beautiful. (4)

Total: 45

Exercise 3.10

1 montes altos amo. (3)

2 regem vidimus. (2)

3 sororem habeo. (2)

4 mater non venit. (3)

5 pater meus bonus est. (3)

6 soror mea dormit. (2)

7 matrem meam amo. (2)

8 mater mea pulchra est. (3)

9 uxor mea timet. (3)

10 parentes nostros amamus. (2)

Total: 25

Exercise 3.11

1 fratrem habeo. (2)

2 soror mea pulchra est. (3)

3 uxor flebat. (2)

4 montes vidimus. (2)

5 parentes dona amant. (3)

6 montes alti sunt. (3)

7 rex donum parentibus suis dedit. (4)

8 et frater et soror currebant. (5)

9 pecuniam patri trado. (3)

10 ceteri discipuli ridebant. (3)

Total: 30

Exercise 3.12

1 rex uxorem habet.

2 puella regem laudat.

3 mater et pater appropinquant.

4 matrem et patrem amo.

5 ad montes currimus.

3 marks for each question. Total: 15

Exercise 3.13

1 Both Marcus and Sextus are Roman boys. (7)

2 Both Valeria and Aurelia are Roman girls. (7)

3 I have both a mother and a father. (5)

4 My sister is both beautiful and famous. (7)

5 The teacher often warns both the boys and the girls. (7)

6 The man both saw and heard the big crowd. (7)

7 I am both laughing and playing. (4)

8 The Romans attacked the town with both spears and arrows. (7)

9 Both the mother and father of the king were angry. (7)

10 My brother is both bad and savage. (7)

Total: 65

Exercise 3.14

1 rex festinabat.	The king was hurrying.	(2 + 2)
2 servus fratrem habebat.	The slave had a brother.	(3 + 3)
3 puella non appropinquabat.	The girl was not approaching.	(2 + 3)
4 donum amavisti.	You liked the present.	(2 + 2)
5 vir feminam punivit.	The man punished the woman.	(3 + 3)

Total: 25

Exercise 3.15

1 montes alti sunt pulchri.	The high mountains are beautiful.	(4 + 4)
2 pueri patres amant.	The boys love their fathers.	(3 + 3)
3 reges sorores habebant.	The kings had sisters.	(3 + 3)
4 uxores bella timent.	The wives are afraid of wars.	(3 + 3)
5 matres discesserunt.	The mothers departed.	(2 + 2)

Total: 30

Exercise 4.1

When the three goddesses came to Jupiter,(6) they said these words:(3) 'Jupiter, we three goddesses want the golden apple.(7) Who is the most beautiful?(3) Choose!(1) Choose now!'(2) Jupiter was frightened.(3) He was afraid of the goddesses' anger.(3) He said,(1) 'Goddesses, you are all very beautiful.(4) You all have beautiful bodies.(4) I cannot choose.(3) However, I know a young man, named Paris.(5) He lives in the city of Troy.(4) He loves beautiful women.(3) He will choose the most beautiful.(3) Ask Paris!'(2)

The three goddesses were angry.(4) However, they decided to ask Paris.(4) And so they went to Paris.(4) The journey was not long.(4) They therefore soon came to Paris.(5) When Paris saw a bright light in the sky,(7) he was afraid.(1) The goddesses told everything about the golden apple.(6) 'Jupiter has sent us to you, Paris.(6) He orders you to choose the most beautiful goddess.(5) Choose now!'(2)

Total: 105

Exercise 4.2

1 (a) ad/in/de. (1)

(b) lege/rogate. (1)

(c) legere/rogare. (1)

(d) aureum/pulcherrima/perterritus/omnes/pulcherrimae/pulchra/pulchras/ pulcherrimam/iratae/longum/claram/omnia/aureo (1)

2 Perfect. dico. (2)

3 Vocative. (1)

4 2nd person Plural Present (3)

Total: 10

Exercise 4.3

1 nomina.

2 iter.

3 corporis.

4 fluminibus.

5 maribus.

6 itineri.

7 nomine.

8 corpora.

9 mare.

10 flumen.

1 mark for each question. Total: 10

Exercise 4.4

1 nomine.

2 nomina.

3 corpora.

4 flumini.

5 mare.

6 itineribus.

7 fluminum.

8 maris.

9 itineri.

10 fluminibus.

Exercise 4.5

1 The sailor is not afraid of the sea. (4)

2 The journey was long and difficult. (5)

3 The slaves were carrying a body. (3)

4 We made many long journeys. (4)

5 The water of the river was deep. (4)

6 There are many temples in the city. (5)

7 I do not like towns and cities. (5)

8 The name of the king was Sextus. (4)

9 My father often sails across the sea alone. (7)

10 The friends were tired from the journey. (4)

Exercise 4.6

1 I saw many bodies in the battle. (5)

2 The journey of the young men was both long and miserable. (7)

3 The king saw a bright light in the sky. (6)

4 The name of the city was Rome. (4)

5 Girls often love beautiful/handsome young men. (5)

6 The father gave much money to the young man. (5)

7 I saw my mother and father in the city yesterday. (6)

8 The body of the sailor was big. (4)

9 We soon came to the river. (4)

10 Tired from the journey, we soon slept. (4)

Exercise 4.7

1 flumen videtis. (2)
2 mare timemus. (2)
3 mare altum est. (3)
4 corpus meum validum est. (4)
5 iter longum erat. (3)
6 nomen non habeo. (3)
7 multa corpora vidi. (3)
8 itinera non saepe facimus. (4)
9 nomen pueri Sextus est. (4)
10 flumina amo. (2)

Total: 30

Exercise 4.8

1 mater flumen timebat. (3)
2 rex iter longum faciebat. (4)
3 in itinere multos iuvenes vidimus. (5)
4 mare nautas non terret. (4)
5 femina corpus pulchrum habebat. (4)

Total: 20

Exercise 4.9

1 puer in flumine stabat.
2 nomen iuvenis Marcus erat.
3 flumina et mare vidimus.
4 aqua fluminis alta erat.
5 undae maris magnae erant.

4 marks for each question. Total: 20

Exercise 4.10

1 matres bonae sunt.	The mothers are good.	(3 + 3)
2 reges bonos laudamus.	We praise the good kings.	(3 + 3)
3 fratres habent.	They have brothers.	(2 + 2)
4 puellae diu currebant.	The girls were running for a long time.	(2 + 3)
5 magistri cucurrerunt.	The teachers ran.	(2 + 2)

Total: 25

Exercise 4.11

1 iuvenis advenit.   The young man arrived.

2 urbem specto.   I am looking at the city.

3 vinum bibebam.   I was drinking wine.

4 corpus portas.   You are carrying the body.

5 lucem vidi.   I saw the light.

2 + 2 marks for each question. Total: 20

Exercise 4.12

1 We were wandering.	1st person	Plural	Imperfect	erro
2 They were/They have been.	3rd person	Plural	Perfect	sum
3 They handed over.	3rd person	Plural	Perfect	trado
4 They approached.	3rd person	Plural	Perfect	appropinquo
5 I announced.	1st person	Singular	Perfect	nuntio

5 marks for each question. Total: 25

Exercise 4.13

1 reximus.   We ruled.

2 erras.   You wander.

3 erant.   They were.

4 tradebam.   I was handing over.

5 scripsistis.   You wrote.

2 marks for each question. Total: 10

Exercise 4.14

1 flumen longum est.	The river is long.	(3 + 3)
2 urbem diu oppugnabas.	You were attacking the city for a long time.	(2 + 3)
3 donum amavi.	I loved the gift.	(2 + 2)
4 puer montem vidit.	The boy saw the mountain.	(3 + 3)
5 poeta narrabat.	The poet was telling.	(2 + 2)

Total: 25

Exercise 4.15

1 iuvenes currunt.	The young men are running.	(2 + 2)
2 itinera longa sunt.	The journeys are long.	(3 + 3)
3 iam advenimus.	We are arriving now.	(1 + 2)
4 reges urbes ceperunt.	The kings captured the cities.	(3 + 3)
5 urbes pulchrae erant.	The cities were beautiful.	(3 + 3)

Total: 25

Exercise 4.16

1 iter longum erat. (3)

2 lucem vidimus. (2)

3 corpus pulchrum habet. (3)

4 servi urbem oppugnaverunt. (3)

5 iuvenes tela iecerunt. (3)

6 nomen regis Marcus est. (4)

7 vir puellam in urbe vidit. (5)

8 in flumine ludimus. (3)

9 nautae mare non timent. (4)

10 periculum filium regis non terret. (5)

Total: 35

Exercise 5.1

Paris was frightened.(3) However, he answered:(2) 'You are all very beautiful, goddesses.(4) I cannot choose now.(4) Return tomorrow!(2) Tomorrow I will decide!'(2)

The goddesses said to Paris,(3) 'We will return tomorrow.'(2) They departed angrily.(2) Juno however approached Paris in secret.(5) She said to Paris,(2) 'If you hand over the apple to me,(5) I will make you the most powerful man.'(4) After she said these words, she departed.(5) Athena also approached Paris in secret.(5) She said to Paris,(2) 'If you choose me,(3) I will make you the wisest man.'(4) After she said these words, she departed.(5) Later Venus approached Paris in secret.(5) She said to Paris,(2) 'If you choose me,(3) I will give you the most beautiful woman as your wife.'(5) Then she departed.(2) Paris was now alone.(4)

Total: 85

Exercise 5.2

1 (a) legere.   (1)

  (b) redite.   (1)

  (c) mihi/ego/te/tu/me/tibi.   (1)

  (d) ad.   (1)

2 Perfect   3rd person   Singular   dico   (4)

3 Accusative. After the preposition ad.   (2)

Total: 10

Exercise 5.3

1 We will carry.

2 He will cry.

3 You will sit.

4 They will kill.

5 I will approach.

6 You will overcome.

7 He will wander.

8 They will hold.

9 You will enter.

10 We will announce.

11 I will cry.

12 We will give.

13 You will tell.

14 You will sail.

15 They will fight.

16 You will laugh.

17 He will see.

18 We will work.

19 You will sing.

20 We will move.

Exercise 5.4

1 They will build.

2 I will order.

3 You will answer.

4 They will stand.

5 We will fight.

6 They will attack.

7 He will shout.

8 You will frighten.

9 They will destroy.

10 You will give.

11 We will approach.

12 He will destroy.

13 I will stay.

14 I will ask.

15 We will laugh.

16 I will see.

17 We will sit.

18 He will stand.

19 You will warn.

20 They will live.

Exercise 5.5

1 stabimus.

2 portabunt.

3 delebo.

4 habebit.

5 appropinquabimus.

6 flebis.

7 superabo.

8 timebunt.

9 vocabimus.

10 pugnabit.

11 respondebo.

12 sedebis.

13 superabunt.

14 ridebit.

15 navigabitis.

Exercise 5.6

1 manebit.

2 oppugnabitis.

3 manebimus.

4 necabis.

5 tenebo.

6 videbimus.

7 spectabunt.

8 flebunt.

9 terrebit.

10 festinabitis.

11 movebo.

12 appropinquabis.

13 tenebimus.

14 intrabitis.

15 rogabunt.

Exercise 5.7

1 We will rule.

2 I will read.

3 You will arrive.

4 I will run.

5 You will hand over.

6 We will decide.

7 You will be.

8 I will flee.

9 They will send.

10 You will want.

11 He will eat.

12 They will be.

13 We will drink.

14 We will run.

15 He will send.

16 We will play.

17 You will read.

18 You will decide.

19 They will play.

20 I will depart.

Exercise 5.8

1 He will flee.

2 You will be.

3 We will write.

4 They will receive.

5 He will sleep.

6 We will depart.

7 They will punish.

8 I will be.

9 I will throw.

10 You will put.

11 We will show.

12 You will sleep.

13 They will run.

14 We will take.

15 He will be.

16 I will sleep.

17 I will come.

18 You will take.

19 You will receive.

20 He will say.

Exercise 5.9

1 He runs.

2 He will run.

3 We rule.

4 We will rule.

5 He will hurry.

6 We hurry.

7 He is.

8 He will be.

9 He will shout.

10 He will drink.

11 He drinks.

12 They will show.

13 They show.

14 He will punish.

15 He punishes.

16 We see.

17 We will see.

18 They will stay.

19 They stay.

20 They will be.

1 mark for each question. Total: 20

Exercise 5.10

1 You will carry.

2 They prepare.

3 I will give.

4 We destroy.

5 We will call.

6 You will destroy.

7 We will sleep.

8 He will tell.

9 They have.

10 You read.

11 We sleep.

12 We enter.

13 You will laugh.

14 You will read.

15 I will have.

16 They will arrive.

17 He will flee.

18 He flees.

19 They take.

20 You will have.

1 mark for each question. Total: 20

Exercise 5.11

1 Yesterday the slave was working. (3)

2 Today the slave is working. (3)

3 Tomorrow the slave will flee. (3)

4 Yesterday we were attacking the town. (3)

5 Today we are attacking the town. (3)

6 Tomorrow we will take the town. (3)

7 Yesterday the boys were running. (3)

8 Today the boys are running. (3)

9 Tomorrow the boys will run. (3)

10 Yesterday I was watching many beautiful girls. (5)

11 Today I am watching many beautiful girls. (5)

12 Tomorrow I will watch many beautiful girls. (5)

13 Yesterday the Romans were carrying shields. (4)

14 Today the Romans are carrying shields. (4)

15 Tomorrow the Romans will not carry shields. (5)

Total: 55

Exercise 5.12

1 multi iuvenes cras advenient. (4)

2 auxilium mox veniet. (3)

3 pater meus iter longum faciet. (5)

4 servi irati muros oppugnabunt. (4)

5 pueri ad ludum festinabunt. (4)

Total: 20

Exercise 5.13

1 vinum cras bibam. (3)

2 discipuli magistros numquam audient. (4)

3 iuvenis ad oppidum festinabit. (4)

4 ancilla cenam numquam iterum parabit. (5)

5 discipuli boni semper laborabunt. (4)

Total: 20

Exercise 5.14

1 ad urbem cras veniam. (4)

2 rex uxorem pulchram habet. (4)

3 femina virum bonum habet. (4)

4 uxor mea cenam bonam parabat. (5)

5 iter nunc facimus. (3)

Total: 20

Exercise 5.15

1 aqua fluminis alta est. (4)

2 uxor regis pecuniam non habebit. (4)

3 de monte venimus. (3)

4 regem in itinere vidistis. (4)

5 quis in urbe cras erit? (5)

Total: 20

Exercise 5.16

1	feminae appropinquant.	The women are approaching.	(2 + 2)
2	discipuli laborabant.	The pupils were working.	(2 + 2)
3	prope flumina mansistis.	You stayed near the rivers	(2 + 3)
4	puellae dona amabant.	The girls loved the gifts.	(3 + 3)
5	iuvenes puellas viderunt.	The young men saw the girls.	(3 + 3)

Total: 25

Exercise 5.17

1	puellam non amo.	I do not love the girl.	(2 + 3)
2	coniugem habeo.	I have a wife.	(2 + 2)
3	advenit.	He arrived.	(1 + 1)
4	puer hastam portabat.	The boy was carrying a spear.	(3 + 3)
5	bene dormivit.	He slept well.	(1 + 2)

Total: 20

Exercise 6.1

On the next day the three goddesses returned.(4) They stood before Paris.(3) 'Paris, you must choose the most beautiful goddess now.'(8)

Although Paris feared the anger of the goddesses, he shouted:(6) 'I choose Venus.(2) Venus is the most beautiful goddess above all the others.'(7)

When Venus heard Paris's words, she laughed.(6) She was happy.(2) When Juno and Athena heard Paris's words, they did not laugh.(9) They were not happy.(3) They departed angrily.(2)

Paris was looking at Venus.(3) 'I have chosen you,' he said.(4) 'I want the most beautiful woman as my wife.(5) Where is she?'(2)

Venus answered Paris:(3) 'The most beautiful woman is Helen.(4) She lives in Greece with her husband Menelaus.(8) Go to Greece, take Helen and return to the city of Troy!(9) In this way the most beautiful woman will be yours.'(5)

Total: 95

Exercise 6.2

1 (a) redierunt/steterunt/clamavit/audivit/risit/audiverunt/riserunt/discesserunt/
respondit. (1)

(b) timebat/erat/erant/spectabat. (1)

(c) ante/in/cum/ad. (1)

2 3rd person   Singular   rideo (3)

3 Neuter. (1)

4 Dative. (1)

5 Accusative. After the preposition ad. (2)

Total: 10

Exercise 6.3

1 I will return.

2 They perished.

3 You were going.

4 They go in.

5 I went.

6 You will go.

7 I go.

8 He goes out.

9 They were going.

10 They will cross.

11 You go.

12 He returned.

28

13 I will go out.

14 They went.

15 They went towards.

Exercise 6.4

1 I perish.

2 You will go.

3 We were going out.

4 He crosses.

5 I returned.

6 They will go out.

7 We were going.

8 He perished.

9 He will return.

10 He was going.

11 He goes towards.

12 We returned.

13 You go.

14 I went out.

15 He went.

Exercise 6.5

1 They crossed.

2 He will go.

3 We go.

4 We will cross.

5 They go.

6 You perish.

7 He was going out.

8 They returned.

9 They will go towards.

10 He will go out.

11 They cross.

12 They will return.

13 We will return.

14 They perish.

15 You were going.

Exercise 6.6

1 We perished.

2 We will go.

3 They go towards.

4 I was going.

5 We go out.

6 They went out.

7 He goes.

8 I will perish.

9 We went.

10 You returned.

11 I cross.

12 We were perishing.

13 We will perish.

14 They willl go.

15 You will go out.

Exercise 6.7

1 imus.

2 ierunt/iverunt.

3 peribant.

4 transeunt.

5 redibimus.

6 inierunt.

7 exii.

8 peribo.

9 redibamus.

10 i!

1 mark for each question. Total: 10

Exercise 6.8

1 exibo.

2 redii.

3 perierunt.

4 exiit.

5 ibatis.

6 transiit.

7 inire.

8 redibant.

9 adibimus.

10 rediit.

1 mark for each question. Total: 10

Exercise 6.9

1 We crossed the river yesterday. (3)

2 We crossed the sea today. (3)

3 I am going to the city. (3)

4 Go, boy! (2)

5 We will go towards the city tomorrow. (4)

6 We were going along the road. (3)

7 Many young men perished. (3)

8 The boys returned soon. (3)

9 Will you return to the city tomorrow? (4)

10 He went out quickly. (2)

Total: 30

Exercise 6.10

1 Who will go to the city tomorrow? (5)

2 Both my brother and I will go to the city tomorrow. (8)

3 Many slaves crossed the river. (5)

4 Many young men perished in the war. (5)

5 Mother and father will soon return to the city. (6)

6 The boy immediately went out of the town. (5)

7 When the man entered the temple, he saw a friend. (7)

8 The sailor, tired from the long journey, finally went towards the city. (8)

9 Many slaves were going along the road. (5)

10 The king ordered the young men to go out of the temple. (6)

Total: 60

Exercise 6.11

1 iuvenis in proelio periit. (4)

2 et mater et pater ad urbem ibant. (7)

3 nauta ab insula rediit. (4)

4 pueri flumen cras transibunt. (5)

5 servi ex oppido heri exierunt. (5)

Total: 25

Exercise 6.12

1 Although the man had much money, he was not happy. (8)

2 Although the waves were big, the sailors were not afraid. (7)

3 Although the king was famous, he did not have a wife. (7)

4 Although the journey was not long, the young men were tired. (8)

5 Although the book is long, it is good. (6)

6 Although the woman is beautiful, she does not have a husband. (7)

7 Although the girls were frightened, they quickly went into the water. (8)

8 Although the slave was tired, he was working well. (6)

9 Although the Greeks fought well, they did not overcome the Romans. (7)

10 Although the Romans were approaching, the king was not afraid. (6)

Total: 70

Exercise 6.13

1 When Paris saw the bright light, he was very afraid. (7)

2 When the slaves saw the master, they were afraid. (5)

3 When the boys heard the words of the teacher, they were happy. (7)

4 When the young man made the long journey, he was tired. (7)

5 When the Romans overcame the Greeks, they captured the city. (6)

6 When we arrived at the city, we hurried to the temple. (7)

7 When I saw my parents, I was happy. (6)

8 When the slaves worked for a long time, they were tired. (6)

9 When the man gave the gift to his wife, he departed. (6)

10 When the sailors arrived at the island, they wanted to look at the city. (8)

Total: 65

Exercise 6.14

1 flumen altum iam transeo. (5)

2 ad urbem imus. (3)

3 multi viri cras peribunt. (4)

4 discipuli magistros numquam amant. (3)

5 femina alta ad templum appropinquat. (5)

Total: 20

Exercise 6.15

1 mater regis pulchra erat. (4)

2 multas hastas habebatis/habuistis. (3)

3 donum iuveni dabo. (3)

4 pueri ab agris ad oppidum currebant. (6)

5 iter ab urbe faciebamus. (4)

Total: 20

Exercise 6.16

1 adibo.   I will go towards.

2 erat.   He was.

3 ierunt/iverunt.   They went.

4 risistis.   You laughed.

5 pugnabas.   You were fighting.

2 marks for each question. Total: 10

Exercise 6.17

1 He will be.	3rd person	Singular	Future	sum
2 You gave.	2nd person	Singular	Perfect	do

3	They will announce.	3rd person	Plural	Future	**nuntio**
4	They arrived.	3rd person	Plural	Perfect	**advenio**
5	We were returning.	1st person	Plural	Imperfect	**redeo**

5 marks for each question. Total: 25

Exercise 6.18

1 Many young men will go to the city tomorrow. (6)
2 Although the woman was beautiful, she did not have a husband. (7)
3 On the journey we saw a bright light. (5)
4 The mother was staying alone in the villa. (5)
5 Both father and mother perished in the war. (7)
6 When we arrived at the city, we stayed there for a long time. (7)
7 Marcus was working. The rest of the pupils were playing near the river. (7)
8 I saw the young man. He was going towards the city. (5)
9 The master will give many gifts to the slaves tomorrow. (6)
10 The wife of the king used to have many slaves. (5)

Total: 60

Exercise 6.19

1	feminae ibant.	The women were going.	(2 + 2)
2	trans flumina transimus.	We are crossing the rivers.	(2 + 3)
3	puellae cras venient.	The girls will come tomorrow.	(2 + 3)
4	ad urbes ibamus.	We were going to the cities.	(2 + 3)
5	iuvenes libros scripserunt.	The young men wrote books.	(3 + 3)

Total: 25

Exercise 6.20

1	ad oppidum adibas.	You were going towards the town.	(2 + 3)
2	mulier pulchra erat.	The woman was beautiful.	(3 + 3)
3	mox adveniam.	I will arrive soon.	(1 + 2)
4	iuvenis periit.	The young man perished.	(2 + 2)
5	etiam servus templum vidit.	Even the slave saw the temple.	(3 + 4)

Total: 25

Exercise 7.1

Helen was a beautiful and famous woman.(6) She lived in the city of Sparta with her husband, named Menelaus.(8) Paris was a famous man.(4) He lived in the city of Troy.(4) Troy was a city situated in Asia.(6)

Paris sailed from the city of Troy to the city of Sparta.(8) When he arrived,(2) Paris disembarked from his ship and hurried to the palace.(8) There he saw the girl Helen.(4) When he saw Helen, he immediately loved her.(6)

Paris said to Helen,(3) 'I love you, Helen.(3) Come!(1) We will sail from the city of Sparta and we will go to the city of Troy!(9) Hurry!'(1)

Paris led Helen to the ship.(5) Then they fled quickly.(3) Paris and Helen sailed to the city of Troy.(7) Paris was happy.(3) Menelaus however, the husband of Helen,(4) was not happy but very angry.(5)

Total: 100

Exercise 7.2

1 (a) ubi/et/sed.   (1)

   (b) ibi/statim/deinde/celeriter.   (1)

2 Ablative. After the preposition **in**.   (2)

3 Ablative.   (1)

4 1st person   Plural   Future   eo   (4)

5 A fugitive is someone who is fleeing, and **fugerunt** means 'they fled'. (1)

Total: 10

Exercise 7.3

1 They flee.   9 He threw.

2 He was crying.   10 We sent.

3 You will attack.   11 We will overcome.

4 They ran.   12 They attacked.

5 They decided.   13 You were running.

6 We will depart.   14 He overcame.

7 You arrived.   15 You wander.

8 He was present.   16 We will sleep.

17 They were/have been.

18 I will decide.

19 He departed.

20 He will give.

1 mark for each question. Total: 20

Exercise 7.4

1 He ordered.

2 I will put.

3 We will flee.

4 We were wanting.

5 He was afraid.

6 He announced.

7 He ruled.

8 I arrive.

9 He led.

10 I order.

11 I will arrive.

12 We move.

13 They send.

14 I handed over.

15 They put.

16 You were attacking.

17 He was saying.

18 They ordered.

19 They wandered.

20 We give.

1 mark for each question. Total: 20

Exercise 7.5

1 You stand.

2 We gave.

3 We were fleeing.

4 He moved.

5 He moves.

6 He was.

7 They were away.

8 We will write.

9 They fled.

10 We will destroy.

11 They departed.

12 They were approaching.

13 He was ruling.

14 I was throwing.

15 He wrote.

16 He handed over.

17 They destroyed.

18 They will be.

19 You cry.

20 He stood.

1 mark for each question. Total: 20

Exercise 7.6

1 adveniemus.

2 cucurrerunt.

3 iussit.

4 constituerunt.

5 spectabant.

6 fugerunt.

7 navigabunt.

8 nuntiavit.

9 vocavit.

10 erant/fuerunt.

11 ierunt/iverunt.

12 ambulabat.

13 navigamus.

14 advenit.

15 curram.

16 pugnaverunt.

17 mittetis.

18 fugiemus.

19 stas.

20 ridebamus.

1 mark for each question. Total: 20

Exercise 7.7

1 aedificabant.

2 ludebamus.

3 iit/ivit.

4 manebis.

5 neco.

6 appropinquabant.

7 bibebamus.

8 tenebat.

9 iaciebamus.

10 rogavit.

11 nuntiabo.

12 responderunt.

13 iubebo.

14 ibant.

15 cepit.

16 lego.

17 eramus/fuimus.

18 misimus.

19 aedificavisti.

20 punivit.

1 mark for each question. Total: 20

Exercise 7.8

1 redibo.

2 audivi.

3 videbimus.

4 dedistis.

5 narraverunt.

6 vidimus.

7 delevit.

8 ero.

9 manserunt.

10 discessimus.

11 discedit.

12 peribatis.

13 scripsi.

14 sumus.

15 constituemus.

16 currebat.

17 iecerunt.

18 pugnabat.

19 delebo.

20 vidit.

1 mark for each question. Total: 20

Exercise 7.9

1 navis appropinquabat. (2)

2 urbem cras oppugnabimus. (3)

3 nautae naves amant. (3)

4 pater pecuniam non habebat/habuit. (4)

5 ceteri discipuli laborabant. (3)

Total: 15

Exercise 7.10

1 mater in nave erat.

2 navem prope insulam vidimus.

3 servi ex urbe fugerunt.

4 naves ad insulam redibant.

5 navis in flumine navigabat.

4 marks for each question. Total: 20

Exercise 7.11

1 iam fugimus. We are already fleeing. (1 + 2)

2 naves pulchrae appropinquabant. Beautiful ships were approaching. (3 + 3)

3 equi dormient. The horses will sleep. (2 + 2)

4 reges terras rexerunt. The kings ruled the lands. (3 + 3)

5 puellae pericula timebant. The girls feared the dangers. (3 + 3)

Total: 25

Exercise 7.12

1 diu currebas. You were running for a long time. (1 + 2)

2 mater misera flebat. The miserable mother was crying. (3 + 3)

3 servus fugit. The slave fled. (2 + 2)

4 agricola agrum habet. The farmer has a field. (3 + 3)

5 discipulus librum legebat. The pupil was reading a book. (3 + 3)

Total: 25

1	narrabat.	He was telling.
2	errabant.	They were wandering.
3	ambulabamus.	We were walking.
4	ridebatis.	You were laughing.
5	timebant.	They were afraid.
6	pugnabat.	He was fighting.
7	manebam.	I was staying.
8	cantabas.	You were singing.
9	videbat.	He was seeing.
10	clamabat.	He was shouting.

2 marks for each question. Total: 20

Exercise 8.1

Menelaus was angry.(3) He was angry because Paris had led his wife, named Helen, to Troy.(10) Menelaus wanted to punish this man and destroy this city.(9)

He therefore sent messengers to all the cities of Greece.(7) These messengers said these words:(5) 'Listen, everyone!(2) Paris has taken Helen, the dear wife of Menelaus.(6) He has fled to Troy.(3) On account of this Menelaus is angry.(5) He wants to destroy this city.(4) Prepare arms!(2) Collect ships and soldiers!(4) We will sail to Troy and punish the Trojans!'(6)

When the Greeks heard these words they prepared many forces.(8) The forces of the Greeks came to a port named Aulis.(7) When Menelaus saw these ships and these soldiers, he was happy.(10) He greeted everyone.(2) He wanted to sail to Troy immediately and to wage war against the Trojans and set Helen free.(12)

Total: 105

Exercise 8.2

1 (a) punire/delere/navigare/gerere/liberare. (1)

(b) ad/propter/contra. (1)

(c) audite/parate/colligite. (1)

(d) navigabimus/puniemus. (1)

2 Accusative. Object of the verb (2)

3 3rd person   Singular   Perfect   mitto (4)

Total: 10

Exercise 8.3

1 This soldier.

2 This king.

3 This shield.

4 This city.

5 These cities.

6 This slave.

7 This mother.

8 These boys.

9 These ships.

10 This gift.

11 These bodies.

12 These kings.

13 These soldiers.

14 This journey.

15 This boy.

16 These slaves.

17 These farmers.

18 This river.

19 These words.

20 This wife.

Exercise 8.4

1 Of this girl.

2 Of this soldier.

3 Of these soldiers.

4 Of these ships.

5 By/with/from this gift.

6 By/with/from this war.

7 By/with/from this light.

8 Of this boy.

9 Of these slaves.

10 To/for/by/with/from these words.

11 By/with/from this sword.

12 To this slave.

13 Of these women.

14 By/with/from this wound.

15 By/with/from this name.

16 To/for/by/with/from these wounds.

17 To/for/by/with/from these names.

18 To/for this young man.

19 To/for/by/with/from these rivers.

20 Of this king.

Exercise 8.5

1 This boy is Marcus. (4)

2 This war is bad. (4)

3 These boys are small. (4)

4 These girls are small. (4)

5 I love this girl. (3)

6 I am listening to these words. (3)

7 The king punishes this soldier. (4)

8 The girl does not like this food. (5)

9 The master will give money to these slaves. (5)

10 These rivers are long. (4)

Total: 40

Exercise 8.6

1 The temple of this god is big. (5)

2 The books of these boys are good. (5)

3 I am giving much money to this boy. (5)

4 I am not giving money to these boys. (5)

5 The teacher kills the boy with this sword. (5)

6 The teacher frightens the boys with these words. (5)

7 I am reading the book of this boy. (4)

8 When the young man heard these words, he departed. (6)

9 The Romans will soon overcome the Greeks with these soldiers. (6)

10 This river is sacred. (4)

Total: 50

Exercise 8.7

1 hic miles.

2 hi milites.

3 haec urbs.

4 hae urbes.

5 hoc flumen.

6 haec flumina.

7 haec arma.

8 hae copiae.

9 haec lux.

10 hoc iter.

2 marks for each question. Total: 20

Exercise 8.8

1 hi iuvenes.

2 haec mater.

3 haec dona.

4 hoc scutum.

5 haec pericula.

6 hic discipulus.

7 hi agri.

8 hic magister.

9 hi muri.

10 haec turba.

2 marks for each question. Total: 20

Exercise 8.9

1 huic puellae.

2 horum agricolarum.

3 huic reginae.

4 hac via.

5 horum Romanorum.

6 his sagittis.

7 hoc cibo.

8 huic equo.

9 horum murorum.

10 huius libri.

2 marks for each question. Total: 20

Exercise 8.10

1 haec navis ad insulam navigabat.

2 hanc puellam pulchram heri vidi.

3 nuntius ad hanc urbem rediit.

4 hoc corpus ex oppido portabam.

5 milites omnia haec arma collegerunt.

5 marks for each question. Total: 25

Exercise 8.11

1 nomen huius puellae Flavia est.

2 muri huius urbis alti sunt.

3 miles hoc gladio bene pugnavit.

4 dominus donum his servis dabit.

5 puellae villam huius iuvenis amabant.

5 marks for each question. Total: 25

Exercise 8.12

1 copiae appropinquabant. (2)

2 dominus servum liberavit. (3)

3 patrem salutavimus. (2)

4 miles bene pugnabat. (3)

5 iuvenis arma colliget. (3)

6 milites multa arma collegerunt. (4)

7 Romani magnas copias habebant. (4)

8 rex militem in proelio necavit. (5)

9 multi milites propter bellum perierunt. (5)

10 arma militum nova erant. (4)

Total: 35

Exercise 8.13

1 liberatis.   You set free.   (1 + 1)

2 milites boni sunt.   The soldiers are good.   (3 + 3)

3 naves cras advenient.   The ships will arrive tomorrow.   (2 + 3)

| 4 | domini servos liberabunt. | The masters will set free the slaves. | (3 + 3) |
| 5 | pueri patres salutaverunt. | The boys greeted their fathers. | (3 + 3) |

Total: 25

Exercise 8.14

1	scutum hastamque collegit.	He collected a shield and spear.	(3 + 3)
2	iuvenis fugiebat.	The young man was fleeing.	(2 + 2)
3	miles pugnabat.	The soldier was fighting.	(2 + 2)
4	mulier cras redibit.	The woman will return tomorrow.	(2 + 3)
5	puella equum amabit.	The girl will love the horse.	(3 + 3)

Total: 25

Exercise 8.15

1	liberavit.	He set free.
2	salutabam.	I was greeting.
3	gessistis.	You did.
4	fugerunt.	They fled.
5	ibimus.	We will go.

2 marks for each question. Total: 10

Exercise 8.16

1	They went out.	3rd person	Plural	Perfect	exeo
2	He was.	3rd person	Singular	Imperfect	sum
3	He did.	3rd person	Singular	Perfect	gero
4	We will drink.	1st person	Plural	Future	bibo
5	I will collect.	1st person	Singular	Future	colligo

5 marks for each question. Total: 25

Exercise 9.1

The Greeks sent many soldiers and many ships to Aulis.[8] When Menelaus caught sight of those soldiers and those ships, he was happy.[10] He did not like Troy.[3] He wanted to destroy that city without delay.[6]

The ships however were not able to sail.[5] The ships were not able to sail because the winds were contrary.[8] The Greeks stayed near their ships for a long time.[5] They were doing nothing.[2] For a long time they waited for favourable winds.[4] No one was happy.[3] But finally the winds were favourable.[5]

Menelaus shouted to the soldiers:[3] 'Companions, those winds are now favourable.[6] Prepare the ships![2] Prepare your weapons![2] We must depart!'[2]

When the Greeks heard these words[5] they quickly prepared the ships[3] and sailed from Aulis.[3]

Total: 85

Exercise 9.2

1 (a) et/ubi/quod/sed. (1)

(b) sine/prope. (1)

(c) miserunt/conspexit/manserunt/exspectaverunt/clamavit/audiverunt/
paraverunt/navigaverunt. (1)

(d) erat/amabat/cupiebat/poterant/erant/faciebant. (1)

2 3rd person   Plural   maneo (3)

3 Accusative. Object of the verb. (2)

4 Neuter. (1)

Total: 10

Exercise 9.3

1 That slave.

2 That ship.

3 That war.

4 Those enemies.

5 Those cities.

6 Those wars.

7 That woman.

8 Those weapons.

9 Those bodies.

10 That river.

11 Those horses.

12 That companion.

13 That girl.

14 Those forces.

15 Those words.

16 That town.

17 That young man.

18 Those companions.

19 That friend.

20 Those soldiers.

2 marks for each question. Total: 40

Exercise 9.4

1 Of that horse.

2 To/for/by/with/from those friends.

3 Of those boys.

4 To/for that woman.

5 In that city.

6 Of those girls.

7 To/for that god.

8 Of those young men.

9 By/with/from that journey.

10 To/for/by/with/from those weapons.

11 To/for/by/with/from those soldiers.

12 To/for that slave.

13 Of those dangers.

14 By/with/from that light.

15 To/for/by/with/from those arrows.

16 Of those teachers.

17 Of that friend.

18 Of those women.

19 Of that city.

20 To/for that slave.

2 marks for each question. Total: 40

Exercise 9.5

1 That slave is good. (4)

2 That girl is beautiful. (4)

3 Those soldiers are tired. (4)

4 That ship is big. (4)

5 That temple is big and beautiful. (6)

6 Those words are bad. (4)

7 I do not like that boy. (4)

8 The master often punishes those slaves. (5)

9 The teacher does not like those girls. (5)

10 The name of that boy is Marcus. (5)

Total: 45

Exercise 9.6

1 The shields of those soldiers are big. (5)

2 I will give money to those slaves tomorrow. (5)

3 The general is giving weapons to that soldier. (5)

4 The boy will kill the beautiful girl with that sword. (6)

5 My mother will love those gifts. (5)

6 I like those words. (3)

7 Many young men live in that city. (4)

8 There are many ships on that river. (5)

9 Where are the books of those boys? (5)

10 That river is sacred. (5)

Total: 50

Exercise 9.7

1 This slave is good, that one is bad. (6)

2 This island is big, that one is small. (6)

3 That slave was afraid of this master. (5)

4 This master was frightening that slave. (5)

5 Those soldiers attacked this city. (5)

6 Those young men were looking at these girls. (5)

7 This ship sailed to that island. (6)

8 Those slaves fled from this town. (6)

9 I saw this girl in that street. (6)

10 That master used to punish these slaves. (5)

Total: 55

Exercise 9.8

1 ille gladius.

2 illa femina/mulier.

3 illud bellum.

4 illi equi.

5 illae puellae.

6 illa templa.

7 illa mora.

8 illi comites.

9 ille miles.

10 illi milites.

2 marks for each question. Total: 20

Exercise 9.9

1 illae naves.

2 illa lux.

3 illud nomen.

4 illa urbs.

5 illi iuvenes.

6 illud iter.

7 illa flumina.

8 illud periculum.

9 ille discipulus.

10 illi libri.

2 marks for each question. Total: 20

Exercise 9.10

1 illius pueri.

2 illius puellae.

3 illius belli.

4 illorum puerorum.

5 illarum puellarum.

6 illorum bellorum.

7 illi servo.

8 illis servis.

9 illis verbis.

10 illo dono.

2 marks for each question. Total: 20

Exercise 9.11

1 illis comitibus.

2 illi militi.

3 illius navis.

4 illa luce.

5 illorum corporum.

6 illis iuvenibus.

7 illi regi.

8 illi urbi.

9 illo nomine.

10 illis amicis.

2 marks for each question. Total: 20

Exercise 9.12

1 illam puellam amo.

2 illas naves specto.

3 illud flumen transeo.

4 illos servos libero.

5 illam urbem oppugno.

3 marks for each question. Total: 15

Exercise 9.13

1 magister illos discipulos non amat. (5)

2 illa navis mox adveniet. (4)

3 dominus pecuniam illis servis numquam dat. (6)

4 dominus illorum servorum malus est. (5)

5 miles amicum illo gladio vulneravit. (5)

Total: 25

Exercise 9.14

1 urbem sine mora oppugnavimus. (4)

2 comites hodie redierunt. (3)

3 nemo navem conspexit. (3)

4 illi milites pugnabant. (3)

5 reginam exspectamus. (2)

Total: 15

Exercise 9.15

1 comites mei mox advenient. (4)

2 rex militem clarum in turba conspexit. (6)

3 puella amicum in oppido diu exspectavit. (6)

4 hunc puerum in urbe vidi. (5)

5 comes meus in bello periit. (4)

Total: 25

Exercise 9.16

1 bella diu gesserunt. They carried on wars for a long time. (2 + 3)

2 matres exspectabant. The mothers were waiting. (2 + 2)

3 comites currebant. The companions were running. (2 + 2)

4 puellae pulchrae erant. The girls were beautiful. (3 + 3)

5 nautae naves conspexerunt. The sailors caught sight of the ships. (3 + 3)

Total: 25

Exercise 9.17

1 frustra fugiebam. I was fleeing in vain. (1 + 2)

2 miles discessit. The soldier departed. (2 + 2)

3 illa navis magna erat. That ship was big. (4 + 4)

4 donum mittam. I will send a gift. (2 + 2)

5 Graecus hastam collegit. The Greek collected a spear. (3 + 3)

Total: 25

Exercise 10.1

Because the winds were favourable,(4) the Greeks prepared their ships.(3) Then they quickly sailed in them across the sea.(7) However, when the ships approached land, no one of the Greeks wanted to disembark from the ships,(13) for the gods had said these words to the Greeks:(6) 'He who disembarks first onto Trojan land will be the first killed.'(9)

For a long time the Greeks did nothing.(4) Among them however was a soldier, named Protesilaus.(7) This soldier was not afraid of death.(5) He shouted:(1) 'Look at me, companions!(3) I am brave.(2) I am daring.(2) I will disembark first onto Trojan land.(5) In this way I will be famous.'(3)

Protesilaus immediately disembarked onto land.(5) When he disembarked, the rest of the Greeks disembarked.(5) After Protesilaus saw the Trojans,(4) he charged against them.(3) He killed many of them.(4) Finally however, after he received many wounds, he perished.(7) In this way he became famous.(3)

Total: 105

Exercise 10.2

1 (a) haec/hic. (1)

  (b) naves/mare/nemo/navibus/miles/nomine/mortem/comites/vulnera. (1)

  (c) primus. (1)

2 **venti** means 'winds' and ventilation means allowing air or wind to circulate. (1)

3 Ablative. After the preposition e. (2)

4 Perfect   facio. (2)

5 Subject: **Protesilaus.**   Object: **Troianos.** (2)

Total: 10

Exercise 10.3

1 Menelaus was a Greek soldier. He was a good man. (8)

2 Helen was the wife of Menelaus. She was a beautiful woman. (8)

3 In the city is a temple. It is a big temple. (8)

4 Marcus has a son. He loves him. (5)

5 Marcus has a daughter. He loves her. (5)

6 Marcus has a son and a daughter. He loves them. (7)

7 Marcus has a slave. He gives money to him. (6)

8 The island is big. Many inhabitants live on it. (8)

9 Marcus receives many books. He always reads them. (7)

10 Marcus has a beautiful wife. Her name is Aurelia. (8)

Total: 70

Exercise 10.4

1 Aurelia has many friends. Her friends are famous. (8)

2 Marcus and Aurelia have many slaves. Their slaves are good. (10)

3 Marcus often gives money to them. (5)

4 Marcus is reading a book. There are many words in it. (8)

5 Marcus sent wine to Aurelia. She is drinking it now. (9)

6 Marcus has many weapons. His weapons are new. (8)

7 Marcus has many weapons. He loves them. (6)

8 The king loves the slaves. He often gives much money to them. (8)

9 The slave asks for water. The master gives it to him. (7)

10 The temple is new. We are looking at it now. (6)

Total: 75

Exercise 10.5

1 The teacher did not like this slave. He therefore used to punish him. (8)

2 Protesilaus was fighting bravely. The Trojans however soon killed him. (8)

3 The Greeks charged against the Trojans. They killed many of them. (8)

4 That soldier received many wounds. His wounds were bad. (9)

5 The master had a good slave, named Sextus. He set him free yesterday. (9)

6 The ship was big. There were many sailors on it. (8)

7 The teacher said many words. However, no one was listening to them. (8)

8 Many girls were approaching. We soon caught sight of them. (6)

9 The Romans were good soldiers. The Greeks did not overcome them. (8)

10 The farmers had many fields. Their fields were big. (8)

Total: 80

Exercise 10.6

1 When his friend came, the man greeted him. (6)

2 My teacher has a beautiful wife. I often see her. (8)

3 That woman was beautiful. Many men loved her.   (8)

4 The city was big. The Romans decided to capture it.   (7)

5 This wine is good. I often drink it.   (7)

6 The Greeks collected many weapons. They put them in the ships.   (8)

7 Meneluas and Helen were Greeks. He was famous, she was beautiful.   (10)

8 Because the slaves were good, the master gave much money to them.   (9)

9 Because he loved the girl, the boy used to give many gifts to her.   (8)

10 With their help we captured the city.   (4)

Total: 75

Exercise 10.7

1 fratrem habeo. eum amo.   (4)

2 sororem habeo. eam amo.   (4)

3 nomen habeo. id non amo.   (5)

4 equos habeo. eos amo.   (4)

5 filias habeo. eas amo.   (4)

6 multa dona habeo. ea amo.   (5)

7 fratrem eius non amo.   (4)

8 puellas amo; matrem earum non amo.   (6)

9 arma eorum nova sunt.   (4)

10 servos habeo. pecuniam eis do.   (5)

Total: 45

Exercise 10.8

1 scripsimus.   We wrote.   (1 + 1)

2 milites perierunt.   The soldiers perished.   (2 + 2)

3 vulnera acceperunt.   They received wounds.   (2 + 2)

4 mulieres dormiebant.   The women were sleeping.   (2 + 2)

5 pueri amicos habent.   The boys have friends.   (3 + 3)

Total: 20

Exercise 10.9

1 comites currunt.   The companiions are running.

2 puellas conspeximus.   We caught sight of the girls.

3 naves exspectabant.   They were waiting for the ships.

4	vulnera accepimus.	We received wounds.	
5	servi ruebant.	The slaves were charging.	

2 + 2 marks for each question. Total: 20

Exercise 10.10

1	amicus fuit.	He was a friend.	(2 + 2)
2	rex currebat.	The king was running.	(2 + 2)
3	militem occidi.	I killed the soldier.	(2 + 2)
4	ancilla scutum non portabat.	The maidservant was not carrying a shield.	(3 + 4)
5	rex comitem occidit.	The king killed his companion.	(3 + 3)

Total: 25

Exercise 10.11

1	Romanus erat.	He was a Roman.	(2 + 2)
2	vulnus malum est.	The wound is bad.	(3 + 3)
3	comes pugnabat.	The companion was fighting.	(2 + 2)
4	servus fugit.	The slave fled.	(2 + 2)
5	ivisti.	You went.	(1 + 1)

Total: 20

Exercise 10.12

1	exspectabant.	They were waiting.
2	conspexit.	He caught sight of.
3	ruam.	I will charge.
4	occidebatis.	You were killing.
5	is.	You go.

2 marks for each question. Total: 10

Exercise 10.13

1	They caught sight of.	3rd person	Plural	Perfect	conspicio
2	You were waiting.	2nd person	Singular	Imperfect	exspecto
3	He will charge.	3rd person	Singular	Future	ruo
4	He kills/killed.	3rd person	Singular	Present/perfect	occido
5	We received.	1st person	Plural	Perfect	accipio

5 marks for each question. Total: 25

Exercise 10.14

1 mortem non timeo.

2 puer donum accepit.

3 Graeci Romanos occident/necabunt.

4 multa vulnera accepimus.

5 comites mei venerunt.

3 marks for each question. Total: 15

Exercise 10.15

1 contra Romanos cras ruemus.   (4)

2 urbem armis oppugnabimus.   (3)

3 mors ad senem mox veniet.   (4)

4 vulnera regis mala sunt.   (3)

5 navis propter moram non hodie advenit.   (6)

Total: 20

Exercise 11.1

Protesilaus was dead.(3) The Greeks charged against the walls of Troy.(5) They fought bravely and for a long time under the walls, but in vain.(8) They did not capture the city.(3) They did not wound many Trojans.(4) They did not kill many Trojans.(4)

Agamemnon, the brother of Menelaus, was the leader of the Greeks.(6) He was not happy.(3) He said these words to the soldiers:(4) 'Greeks, I say these words to you:(5) we will not capture Troy today.(4) The walls of Troy are high and strong.(6) Those Trojan citizens are brave.(5) They defend the walls well.(3) I order you to pitch camp.(4) Sleep well!(2) Tomorrow we will have to fight against the enemy again.'(5)

The Greek soldiers obeyed Agamemnon's words.(5) They pitched camp.(2) They were tired.(2) Soon they were asleep.(2)

Total: 85

Exercise 11.2

1 (a) fortiter/diu/frustra/non/hodie/bene/cras/iterum/mox.   (1)

  (b) Troiae/Menelai/Graecorum/Agamemnonis.   (1)

  (c) ponere pugnare.   (1)

2 mortuus means 'dead' and a mortuary is where dead bodies are stored.   (1)

3 Accusative. After the preposition contra.   (2)

4 capio.   (1)

5 1st person   Plural   Future   (3)

Total: 10

Exercise 11.3

1 You are playing; I am working.   (4)

2 We are Romans; you are Greeks.   (6)

3 We do not like you.   (4)

4 You do not like us.   (4)

5 I do not like you.   (4)

6 You do not like me.   (4)

7 No one saw me.   (3)

8 I love the girl.   (3)

9 The girl does not love me. (4)

10 I saw you in the city. (4)

Total: 40

Exercise 11.4

1 The enemy are attacking us. (3)

2 The Romans do not like us. (4)

3 My father likes you. (4)

4 I will punish you, slave! (3)

5 Who is calling me? (3)

6 The teacher is calling you. (3)

7 The woman is looking at us. (3)

8 Who will give me money? (4)

9 I will give you much money. (5)

10 The girls will play with us. (3)

Total: 35

Exercise 11.5

1 The slave is standing near me. (4)

2 The enemy are fighting against us. (4)

3 Father gives money to you. (4)

4 The master will give money to you, slaves. (5)

5 The slaves are hurrying towards me. (4)

6 Friends are playing with me. (3)

7 I will give a gift to you. (4)

8 The teacher never gives gifts to us. (5)

9 Father gave a gift to me, money to you. (6)

10 That teacher likes you, not me. (6)

Total: 45

Exercise 11.6

1 ego Romanus sum; tu Graecus es. (6)

2 nos boni sumus; vos mali estis. (6)

3 ego pecuniam tibi do. (4)

4 pecuniam nobis saepe dat. (4)

5 mecum ludite, amici! (3)

6 tecum ludere non cupimus. (3)

7 illa puella donum mihi numquam dabit. (6)

8 magister te, sed non me, puniet. (6)

9 hoc nobis facit. (4)

10 nobiscum veni, mater! (3)

Total: 45

Exercise 11.7

1 vos cras videbimus.	We will see you tomorrow.	(2 + 3)
2 hastae servos vulneraverunt.	Spears wounded the slaves.	(3 + 3)
3 reges mortui erant.	The kings were dead.	(3 + 3)
4 milites naves exspectabant.	The soldiers were waiting for the ships.	(3 + 3)
5 duces bella non timent.	Leaders do not fear wars.	(3 + 4)

Total: 30

Exercise 11.8

1 puer mortuus non currit.	The dead boy is not running.	(3 + 4)
2 cur me monebis?	Why will you warn me?	(2 + 3)
3 miles regem vulnerabat.	The soldier was wounding the king.	(3 + 3)
4 civis oppidum defendit.	The citizen defended the town.	(3 + 3)
5 dux comitem amabat.	The leader liked his companion.	(3 + 3)

Total: 30

Exercise 11.9

1 Those soldiers fought bravely in the battle. (6)

2 I caught sight of this citizen in the city yesterday. (6)

3 Many ships were defending the island against the enemy. (6)

4 Because the soldiers were fighting well, the general praised them. (7)

5 The Romans often used to wage wars against the Greeks. (6)

6 The weapons of the Roman soldiers were new. (5)

7 The companions departed from the island in ships without delay. (8)

8 The enemy wounded many citizens with their weapons. (5)

9 Because I never used to work, that teacher did not like me. (9)

10 The forces of the enemy received many wounds from us. (7)

Total: 65

Exercise 11.10

1 civis Romanus mortuus erat. (4)

2 contra hostes pugnabamus. (3)

3 cives boni urbem bene defenderunt. (5)

4 hastae milites vulneraverunt. (3)

5 hostes bene diu pugnabant. (4)

6 cives ad urbem festinaverunt. (4)

7 hostes regem sagittis vulneraverunt. (4)

8 duces boni mortem non timent. (5)

9 hostes in urbe vidimus. (4)

10 vulnera civis mala erant. (4)

Total: 40

Exercise 12.1

The Greeks had attacked Troy.[(3)] However, they had not seized the city of Troy immediately.[(6)] They had not conquered the Trojans.[(3)] They had therefore pitched camp near the city of Troy.[(6)]

For a long time the forces of the Greeks were attacking the walls of Troy.[(6)] However, they were not able to destroy them.[(5)] All the Greeks therefore were very angry, the Trojans very happy.[(7)]

Priam was the king of Troy.[(4)] He had many brave children.[(4)] No one, however, was braver or more famous than Hector.[(8)] He was a man of great courage.[(4)] He used to fight bravely for the Trojans.[(4)]

Among the Greeks also there were many brave soldiers.[(7)] Achilles, however, was the bravest.[(4)] Achilles had a friend named Patroclus.[(5)] Because Hector had killed Patroclus in battle, Achilles was very angry.[(9)]

Total: 85

Exercise 12.2

1 (a) non/statim/diu/fortiter. (1)

   (b) prope/pro/inter/in. (1)

   (c) delere. (1)

2 Subject: **Graeci.**   Object: **Troiam.** (2)

3 **sum.** (1)

4 Genitive. (1)

5 3rd person   Singular   Imperfect (3)

Total: 10

Exercise 12.3

1 amaverat.

2 portaverant.

3 manseramus.

4 videram.

5 miseras.

6 posuerant.

7 feceramus.

8 ceperatis.

9 audiverant.

10 veneram.

11 dormiverat.

12 puniverat.

13 luseras.

14 dederat.

15 riserant.

16 pugnaveramus.

17 discesserant.

18 legeram.

19 deleveramus.

20 ambulaverat.

Exercise 12.4

1 fecerant.

2 viderat.

3 deleveras.

4 posueramus.

5 riseram.

6 puniveratis.

7 fecerat.

8 miserat.

9 veneramus.

10 ceperant.

Exercise 12.5

1 We had loved.

2 They had taken.

3 You had heard.

4 He had ruled.

5 I had given.

6 He had led.

7 We had moved.

8 He had frightened.

9 They had answered.

10 I had sent.

Exercise 12.6

1 He had put.

2 They had run.

3 You had departed.

4 I had read.

5 We had slept.

6 We had walked.

7 He had fled.

8 You had made.

9 We had laughed.

10 You had destroyed.

Exercise 12.7

1 We had stayed.

2 They had seen.

3 He had fought.

4 They had entered.

5 He had taken.

6 You had warned.

7 He had drunk.

8 He had said.

9 We had played.

10 You had killed.

1 The teacher was angry because we had laughed. (5)

2 The boy had not read the book. (4)

3 The boys had been bad. (3)

4 The girl had wounded the boy. (3)

5 We had not heard the words. (3)

6 The master was happy because he had slept well. (6)

7 The slaves had worked well. (3)

8 His wife had departed. (5)

9 The slave had prepared food. (3)

10 A friend had given much money to him. (5)

Total: 40

1 The enemy were happy because the Romans had departed. (6)

2 The gods had conquered the Romans. (3)

3 They had never destroyed the city. (3)

4 We had arrived quickly. (2)

5 They had captured many towns. (3)

6 The boy was running quickly because he had seen the angry teacher. (7)

7 The angry teacher had caught sight of him. (4)

8 The strong soldier had frightened him. (4)

9 Finally he had killed the general. (4)

10 The wicked slave had wounded his sister. (4)

Total: 40

1 The boy had worked for a long time. (3)

2 The general had been angry. (3)

3 The soldiers had fought well. (3)

4 I had slept well. (2)

5 The miserable boy had not laughed. (4)

6 The battle had been long. (3)

7 The enemy had overcome many lands. (4)

8 The master had set free many slaves. (4)

9 The king of the enemy had hurried to the river. (5)

10 The soldiers had attacked the town bravely. (4)

Total: 35

Exercise 12.11

1 The slaves had run out of the town. (4)

2 The teacher had read many books. (4)

3 The messenger had said many words. (4)

4 The slave had drunk much water. (4)

5 The woman had received many wounds. (4)

6 The boy had sent a gift to his father. (5)

7 The soldiers had crossed the river. (4)

8 We had not caught sight of the girl. (3)

9 The soldiers had not fought well. (4)

10 The citizens had defended the town bravely. (4)

Total: 40

Exercise 12.12

1 hostes viceramus.

2 urbem occupaverant.

3 regem vulneraverat.

4 oppidum defenderamus.

5 puellam videram.

2 marks for each question. Total: 10

Exercise 12.13

1 dux multa verba dixerat.

2 miles amicum hasta vulneraverat.

3 hostes contra oppidum ruerant.

4 nautae navem diu exspectaverant.

5 Graeci multa arma collegerant.

4 marks for each question. Total: 20

Exercise 12.14

1 occupant.

2 defendebamus.

3 vincetis.

They seize.

We were defending.

You will conquer.

4 vulneravisti.   You wounded.

5 vicit.   He conquered.

2 marks for each question. Total: 10

Exercise 12.15

1	We will defend.	1st person	Plural	Future	defendo
2	He was going.	3rd person	Singular	Imperfect	eo
3	He had conquered.	3rd person	Singular	Pluperfect	vinco
4	You will be.	2nd person	Plural	Future	sum
5	He wounded.	3rd person	Singular	Perfect	vulnero

5 marks for each question. Total: 25

Exercise 12.16

1	duces clari erant.	The generals were famous.	(3 + 3)
2	urbes defenditis.	You are defending the cities.	(2 + 2)
3	domini servos vulneraverant.	The masters had wounded the slaves.	(3 + 3)
4	reges numquam conspeximus.	We never caught sight of the kings.	(2 + 3)
5	oppida occupabimus.	We will seize the towns.	(2 + 2)

Total: 25

Exercise 12.17

1	vincam.	I will conquer.	(1 + 1)
2	hasta vulnerat.	The spear wounds.	(2 + 2)
3	dux pugnaverat.	The general had fought.	(2 + 2)
4	Romanum vici.	I conquered the Roman.	(2 + 2)
5	civis mortuus erat.	The citizen was dead.	(3 + 3)

Total: 20

Exercise 12.18

1 virtutem non habeo.

2 hostes saevi erant.

3 hostes numquam superabimus/
vincemus.

4 oppidum cras occupabunt.

5 Romani Graecos vicerunt.

3 marks for each question. Total: 15

Exercise 12.19

1 ille vir magnam virtutem habet. (5)

2 virtus militum illorum clara erat. (4)

3 hi cives oppidum bene defendebant. (5)

4 milites urbem magna virtute oppugnabant. (5)

5 comitem meum in urbe heri vidi. (6)

Total: 25

Exercise 12.20

1 occupabant	They were seizing.
2 vulnerabat	He was wounding.
3 exspectabamus	We were waiting.
4 manebamus	We were staying.
5 liberabatis	You were setting free.
6 ridebat	He was laughing.
7 salutabant	They were greeting.
8 respondebat	He was answering.
9 rogabat	He was asking.
10 dabam	I was giving.

2 marks for each question. Total: 20

Exercise 13.1

Achilles was angry because Hector had killed Patroclus.(7) He therefore wanted to kill Hector.(4)

One day the Trojans were fighting against the Greeks near the city of Troy.(8) Everyone was fighting bravely.(3) Then suddenly Achilles by chance caught sight of Hector.(6) When he saw him, he shouted to him:(5) 'Listen to me, Hector!(3) I am Achilles, the bravest of the Greeks.(5) You are a cruel man.(4) Because you killed my friend Patroclus, I will kill you!'(8)

When Hector heard Achilles' words, he answered him:(7) 'Listen to my words, Achilles!(4) I am happy because I have killed your friend Patroclus.(7) I am not frightened of you.(4) You do not frighten me.(4) You are not brave.(3) You are not daring.(3) Come!(1) Fight!(1) Victory will be easy for me.(4) I will soon conquer you!'(4)

Total: 95

Exercise 13.2

1 (a) occiderat. (1)

(b) audi/veni/pugna. (1)

(c) eum/ei/me/ego/tu/te/mihi. (1)

(d) occidam/erit/vincam. (1)

2 Accusative. After the preposition **prope**. (2)

3 Perfect. **conspicio**. (2)

4 Exclamation means 'shouting out' and **clamavit** means 'he shouted.' (1)

5 Neuter. (1)

Total: 10

Exercise 13.3

1 A noble king.

2 Noble kings.

3 A difficult task.

4 Difficult tasks.

5 Brave soldiers.

6 All the shields.

7 All the girls.

8 Sad men.

9 A brave soldier.

10 Cruel wounds.

11 A difficult son.

12 A difficult journey.

13 Cruel masters.

14 A sad girl.

15 A noble general.

2 marks for each question. Total: 30

Exercise 13.4

1 All rivers.

2 All spears.

3 A brave general.

4 Brave generals.

5 Cruel women.

6 The brave enemy.

7 An easy task.

8 A difficult book.

9 Noble men.

10 A difficult road.

11 Cruel words.

12 A cruel word.

13 Sad slaves.

14 A noble name.

15 The sad mother.

2 marks for each question. Total: 30

Exercise 13.5

1 I have a cruel master.

2 I am doing an easy task.

3 I love all wines.

4 I read all books.

5 I am looking at all the girls.

6 I am not carrying everything.

7 I am reading a difficult book.

8 I praise the brave general.

9 I see the sad slave.

10 I praise all the boys.

3 marks for each question. Total: 30

Exercise 13.6

1 I am setting free the brave slave.

2 I love all the girls.

3 I do not love everyone.

4 I like difficult tasks.

5 I am killing the cruel master.

6 I fear cruel soldiers.

7 I praise the brave soldiers.

8 I am doing a difficult task.

9 I am carrying all the weapons.

10 I hear the cruel words.

3 marks for each question. Total: 30

Exercise 13.7

1 This soldier is brave and strong. (6)

2 These soldiers are brave and strong. (5)

3 That girl is noble. (4)

4 This book is difficult. (4)

5 My master is cruel. (4)

6 All the boys are working. (3)

7 Why are you sad, boy? (4)

8 I am sad because the teacher is cruel. (6)

9 Not all tasks are difficult. (5)

10 This king is noble. (4)

Total: 45

Exercise 13.8

1 The cruel teacher punishes all the boys. (5)

2 We are reading an easy book. (3)

3 I do not like this difficult task. (5)

4 All the girls are playing. (3)

5 Not all teachers are cruel. (5)

6 The sad slaves are afraid of the cruel master. (5)

7 The noble master praises the slaves. (4)

8 My brother is preparing everything. (4)

9 We often make difficult journeys. (4)

10 The slaves are sad because the master is often cruel. (7)

Total: 45

Exercise 13.9

1 iter facile.

2 libri difficiles.

3 bellum difficile.

4 puella tristis.

5 domini crudeles.

6 omnes milites.

7 opus facile.

8 miles fortis.

9 feminae/mulieres tristes.

10 omnia vina.

2 marks for each question. Total: 20

Exercise 13.10

1 via facili.

2 puero crudeli.

3 militibus fortibus.

4 omnium puellarum.

5 vulnere crudeli.

6 domino nobili.

7 omnibus hastis.

8 pueri fortis.

9 puellae nobili.

10 libro tristi.

2 marks for each question. Total: 20

Exercise 13.11

1 regina nobilis tristis erat. (4)

2 omnes pueri vinum amant. (4)

3 rex crudelis militem fortem punivit. (5)

4 omnia bella crudelia sunt. (4)

5 iter non facile sed difficile erat. (6)

6 milites bene pugnaverant. (3)

7 omnes hostes superabimus/vincemus. (3)

8 omnes cives timebant. (4)

9 dominum crudelem non amamus. (4)

10 ille rex nobilis est. (4)

11 vulnera omnium civium mala sunt. (5)

12 omnes discipuli bene laboraverunt. (4)

13 bene laborare non facile est. (5)

14 civis fortis contra hostes pugnavit. (5)

15 ad urbem itinere facili venimus. (5)

Total: 65

Exercise 13.12

1 rident. They laugh. (1 + 1)

2 matres non timebant. The mothers were not afraid. (2 + 3)

3 pueri patres habent. The boys have fathers. (3 + 3)

4 milites urbes oppugnaverunt. The soldiers attacked the cities. (3 + 3)

5 discipuli magistros audiebant. The pupils were listening to the teachers. (3 + 3)

Total: 25

Exercise 13.13

1 sagitta vulnerat. The arrow wounds. (2 + 2)

2 servus oppidum delevit. The slave destroyed the town. (3 + 3)

3 dominus servum punivit. The master punished the slave. (3 + 3)

4 oppidum diu defendebam. I was defending the town for a long time. (2 + 3)

5 vir currebat. The man was running. (2 + 2)

Total: 25

Exercise 14.1

Achilles was looking at Hector.(3) Hector was looking at Achilles.(3) Hector was a brave and daring man.(6) Achilles, however, was braver and more daring than Hector.(8)

Suddenly Hector threw his spear.(4) The spear flew towards Achilles.(4) However, it stuck in Achilles' shield.(5) When Achilles saw this, he laughed.(5) Then he said these cruel words to Hector:(6) 'You have not killed me, Hector.(4) I am braver than you.(4) I am the bravest of all the Greeks.(4) Now I will kill you.'(3)

When he said these words,(3) he threw his spear at Hector.(4) The spear stuck in Hector's body.(5) Hector fell to the ground, dead.(5) Achilles was very happy.(3) He laughed.(1)

Total: 80

Exercise 14.2

1 (a) tu/me/ego/te. (1)

   (b) fortis/audax/fortior/audacior/suum/crudelia/fortissimus/
       omnium/mortuus/laetissimus. (1)

2 Subject: **Achilles.**   Object: **Hectorem.** (2)

3 3rd person   Singular   Perfect   **iacio** (4)

4 Accusative. After the preposition **ad.** (2)

Total: 10

Exercise 14.3

1 The brave soldier.

2 The cruel master.

3 The huge temple.

4 The lucky boys.

5 Wise teachers.

6 Wise words.

7 A daring general.

8 A sad war.

9 Difficult battles.

10 A lucky slave.

2 marks for each question. Total: 20

Exercise 14.4

1 A huge task.

2 Difficult masters.

3 Cruel brothers.

4 Daring enemy.

5 All the soldiers.

6 All the words.

7 A wise word.

8 Huge temples.

9 Brave slaves.

10 The daring king.

2 marks for each question. Total: 20

Exercise 14.5

1 The cruel master punishes all the slaves. (5)

2 All the soldiers are brave. (4)

3 Not all wars are wise. (5)

4 I never read difficult books. (4)

5 We are building a huge temple. (3)

6 Rome was a huge city. (4)

7 A wise general always praises brave soldiers. (6)

8 Not all kings are cruel. (5)

9 We are making a long and difficult journey. (5)

10 The teacher praises the wise boy. (4)

Total: 45

Exercise 14.6

1 All the Roman soldiers were daring. (5)

2 The sister of the girl is lucky. (4)

3 All teachers are wise. (4)

4 That girl has a wise brother. (5)

5 Soldiers always like a lucky general. (5)

6 The slaves are doing a difficult task. (4)

7 All slaves work well. (4)

8 We like the wise father of that girl. (5)

9 We came/we are coming to the city by an easy journey. (4)

10 We will soon capture all the soldiers. (4)

Total: 45

Exercise 14.7

1 ille miles altus audax est. (5)

2 patrem sapientem habeo. (3)

3 milites duces felices amant. (4)

4 non omnes viri sapientes sunt. (5)

5 hostes fortes erant. (3)

Total: 20

Exercise 14.8

1 This soldier is brave; that soldier is braver. (8)

2 That soldier is braver than this soldier. (7)

3 That spear is long; this spear is longer. (8)

4 This spear is longer than that one. (6)

5 That girl is wiser than this boy. (7)

6 Teachers are wiser than boys. (5)

7 Teachers are often very wise. (4)

8 This temple is higher than that. (6)

9 This task is not easy but very difficult. (7)

10 Roman soldiers were braver than Greek soldiers. (7)

Total: 65

Exercise 14.9

1 Soldiers are more daring than citizens. (5)

2 That girl is very beautiful; I have never seen a more beautiful girl. (8)

3 That teacher was very angry; I have never seen a more angry teacher. (8)

4 That soldier was very bold; I have never seen a more bold soldier. (8)

5 That woman was very sad; I have never seen a sadder woman. (8)

6 Achilles was a very brave but very cruel soldier. (6)

7 The Romans were more daring than the Greeks. (5)

8 Greek cities were more beautiful than Roman cities. (7)

9 All women are wiser than men. (6)

10 The Romans were famous, but the Greeks were more famous than the Romans. (9)

Total: 70

Exercise 14.10

1 vir sapientissimus.

2 murus altissimus.

3 milites audacissimi.

4 rex felicissimus.

5 dominus crudelissimus.

6 flumina longissima.

7 iter difficillimum.

8 uxor carissima.

9 templum sacerrimum.

10 opera facillima.

2 marks for each question. Total: 20

Exercise 14.11

1 verbis laetissimis.

2 in muro altiore.

3 magistro iratissimo.

4 pueris felicissimis.

5 viri sapientioris.

6 puella pulchriore.

7 regi clarissimo.

8 dominorum crudelissimorum.

9 bello longissimo.

10 itinere faciliore.

2 marks for each question. Total: 20

Exercise 14.12

1 filius meus altissimus et clarissimus est. (6)

2 Marcus sapientior est quam Flavia. (5)

3 pueri sapientiores sunt quam puellae. (5)

4 illud templum altius est quam hoc. (6)

5 puellas pulcherrimas specto. (3)

Total: 25

Exercise 14.13

1 dederunt.	They gave.	(1 + 1)
2 magna tela habemus.	We have big missiles.	(3 + 3)
3 milites audaces sunt.	The soldiers are daring.	(3 + 3)
4 viri non festinabunt.	The men will not hurry.	(2 + 3)
5 iuvenes gladios habebant.	The young men had swords.	(3 + 3)

Total: 25

Exercise 14.14

1 non curram.	I will not run.	(1 + 2)
2 servus felix erat.	The slave was lucky	(3 + 3)
3 hasta militem vulneravit.	The spear wounded the soldier.	(3 + 3)
4 iuvenis telum timebat.	The young man was afraid of the missile.	(3 + 3)
5 iter longum et difficile est.	The journey is long and difficult.	(4 + 5)

Total: 30

Exercise 14.15

1	ibas.	You were going.
2	vincimus.	We conquer.
3	vulneraverunt.	They wounded.
4	manserat.	He had stayed.
5	discessi.	I departed.

2 marks for each question. Total: 10

Exercise 14.16

1 You charge.	2nd person	Singular	Present	**ruo**
2 They seize.	3rd person	Plural	Present	**occupo**
3 He was receiving.	3rd person	Singular	Imperfect	**accipio**
4 They will defend.	3rd person	Plural	Future	**defendo**
5 He had conquered.	3rd person	Singular	Pluperfect	**vinco**

5 marks for each question. Total: 25

Exercise 14.17

1 ille dux audax erat. (4)

2 amicum felicem habeo. (3)

3 dux multa tela iecit. (4)

4 viri sapientes mortem saepe timent. (5)

5 multa tela ducem vulneraverunt. (4)

Total: 20

Exercise 14.18

1 tela hostium longa erant.

2 muri oppidi ingentes erant.

3 urbem multis telis oppugnavimus.

4 virtus civis regem terruit.

5 virtus militum magna erat.

4 marks for each question. Total: 20

Exercise 15.1

Achilles was a very cruel man.(4) He tied Hector's body to his own chariot by his feet. (6) Then he drove the chariot around the walls of Troy,(6) dragging Hector's body.(3) When all the Trojan citizens saw this,(6) they were very sad.(2)

Paris was a son of Priam.(4) He was therefore Hector's brother.(4) Because Achilles had killed Hector,(4) he was very angry.(2) He took his weapons,(2) ran out of the city(3) and charged into battle.(3) He soon found Achilles.(3) He said these words to him:(4) 'Achilles, you are a very wicked man.(4) No one is more wicked than you.(5) You killed Hector, my brother.(4) I however am a better soldier than you.(7) You will never escape.(2) No one will be able to save you.(4) I will kill you now.'(3) Paris threw a missile at Achilles.(5) The missile stuck in Achilles' heel.(5) Achilles fell to the ground, dead.(5)

Total: 100

Exercise 15.2

1 (a) crudelissimus/tristissimi/iratissimus/pessimus. (1)

(b) circum/ex/in/ad. (1)

(c) occiderat. (1)

(d) deinde/mox/numquam/nunc. (1)

2 Subject: Achilles.
Object: Hectorem. (2)

3 Ablative. After the preposition ex. (2)

4 Perfect. mitto. (2)

Total: 10

Exercise 15.3

1 I am a good boy, but you are better. (8)

2 Sextus is a very bad boy. (4)

3 Julius Caesar was a very good general. (5)

4 This temple is bigger than that one. (6)

5 Alexander the Great was a better soldier than Julius Caesar. (8)

6 The food of your mother was very good. (5)

7 Very big ships were approaching. (3)

8 I have more money than you. (6)

9 Italy is bigger than Britain. (5)

10 Britain is smaller than Italy. (5)

Total: 55

Exercise 15.4

1 That girl is very small. (4)

2 This boy is bigger than that girl. (7)

3 Very many soldiers attacked the town. (4)

4 That teacher was very bad. (4)

5 Girls are better than boys. (5)

6 Boys are worse than girls. (5)

7 Roman soldiers were the best. (4)

8 The Romans had better soldiers than the Greeks. (6)

9 The Greeks had worse soldiers than the Romans. (6)

10 Very many citizens were defending the very big town. (5)

Total: 50

Exercise 15.5

1 My wound is very bad. (4)

2 I have never received a worse wound. (4)

3 The mountains of Italy are bigger than the mountains of Britain. (7)

4 The walls of Troy were once very big. (5)

5 The soldiers were in very great danger. (5)

6 This farmer has very many and very big fields. (7)

7 There are very many horses in the fields. (5)

8 I have never been in a bigger ship than that one. (7)

9 The Greeks used to build bigger and better temples than the Romans. (8)

10 The temples of the Romans were smaller and worse than the Greeks'. (8)

Total: 60

Exercise 15.6

1 puer pessimus.

2 discipuli optimi.

3 plurimi milites.

4 plurimae naves.

5 duces optimi.

6 templum maius.

7 urbs minima.

8 bella maxima.

9 puellae minores.

10 magister optimus.

Exercise 15.7

1 non omnes magistri optimi sunt. (5)

2 paucos discipulos pessimos habeo. (4)

3 scuta maxima portamus. (3)

4 illa puella minima erat. (4)

5 navem maiorem numquam vidi. (4)

Exercise 15.8

1 A very good teacher.

2 A very deep river.

3 A very bad pupil.

4 A very brave soldier.

5 Very brave soldiers.

6 A very beautiful girl.

7 A very big town.

8 Very many boys.

9 A very big crowd.

10 A very small river.

11 The very daring enemy.

12 The very bad slaves.

13 A very difficult book.

14 A very cruel master.

15 A very noble man.

16 The best wine.

17 The best soldiers.

18 A very long book.

19 A very good book.

20 Very long rivers.

Exercise 15.9

1 A very beautiful wife.

2 Very wise words.

3 Very big ships.

4 The very savage enemy.

5 Very beautiful women.

6 Very big bodies.

7 Very big temples.

8 A very big temple.

9 A very big shield.

10 Very happy boys.

11 Very many women.

12 Very deep water.

13 A very lucky boy.

14 A very cruel woman.

15 Very big forces.

16 A very long road.

17 A very handsome man.   19 A very big field.

18 A very beautiful sky.   20 A very angry teacher.

2 marks for each question. Total: 40

Exercise 15.10

1 effugiebant.	They were escaping.	(1 + 1)
2 milites pugnabant.	The soldiers were fighting.	(2 + 2)
3 libros nostros tandem invenimus.	We finally found our books.	(3 + 4)
4 cives tuti sunt.	The citizens are safe.	(3 + 3)
5 puellae iuvenes timebant.	The girls were afraid of the young men.	(3 + 3)

Total: 25

Exercise 15.11

1 defendis.	You defend.	(1 + 1)
2 navis veniebat.	The ship was coming.	(2 + 2)
3 servus effugit.	The slave escaped.	(2 + 2)
4 civis urbem servabat.	The citizen was saving the city.	(3 + 3)
5 corpus invenit.	He found a body.	(2 + 2)

Total: 20

Exercise 15.12

1 Very many slaves were afraid of the enemy and were escaping from the city. (8)

2 The Romans used to do more difficult tasks than the Greeks. (6)

3 Although the general had conquered many enemies, no one praised him. (8)

4 All soldiers fear death in war. (6)

5 Greek citizens were wiser than Roman citizens. (7)

6 The Roman soldiers had taken many towns and had conquered many enemies. (9)

7 I caught sight of very many very beautiful girls in the city yesterday. (7)

8 Roman soldiers always used to fight bravely for Roman citizens. (8)

9 These slaves had a very cruel master. They did not like him. (8)

10 The citizens were defending the walls of the town against the enemy with the greatest bravery. (8)

Total: 75

Exercise 15.13

1 circum murum curro. (3)

2 pecuniam in via inveni. (4)

3 servi felices effugerunt. (3)

4 rex multam pecuniam servavit. (4)

5 dux oppidum occupavit. (3)

6 murus ingens urbem servavit. (4)

7 Romani Graecos armis vicerunt. (4)

8 agricola equum in agro invenit. (5)

9 arma Romanorum hostes terruerunt. (4)

10 miles fortis amicum suum in proelio servat. (6)

Total: 40

Exercise 16.1

The Greeks had attacked the city of Troy for a long time.(5) After many years they were tired.(5) Although they used to fight bravely, they were not able to take the city.(7) 'What will we do?' they said.(3) 'We won't capture the city, will we?(3) The walls of Troy are very high and very big.(6) We will never be able to destroy them.(4) We ought to return home'.(3)

When Ulysses, the most daring soldier of the Greeks, heard these words, he was angry.(9) He shouted in a loud voice:(3) 'Listen to me, Greeks!(3) Don't be stupid!(3) We Greeks are wiser than those Trojans.(6) You must not return home! (3) We will soon capture Troy.(3) I have a plan.(2) I have a very good plan.(3) By my plan we will destroy the city.(4) Build a very big wooden horse!'(4) The Greeks therefore built a very big wooden horse.(6)

Total: 85

Exercise 16.2

1 (a) altissimi/maximi/audacissimus/optimum/maximum.   (1)

  (b) sapientiores.   (1)

  (c) audite/nolite/aedificate.   (1)

  (d) diu/fortiter/non/numquam/mox.   (1)

2 Accusative. Object of the verb.   (2)

3 Masculine.   (1)

4 1st person   Plural   Future   (3)

Total: 10

Exercise 16.3

1 He is able/He can.

2 You are able/You can.

3 He was able/He could.

4 He had been able.

5 He will be able.

6 We have been able/We could.

7 To be able.

8 You had been able.

9 You were able/You could.

10 You are able/You can.

11 I am able/I can.

12 We were able/We could.

13 He has been able/He could.

14 They have been able/They could.

15 We had been able.

16 They are able/They can.

17 They will be able.

18 We are able/We can.

19 You have been able/You could.

20 I will be able.

1 mark for each question. Total: 20

Exercise 16.4

1 I cannot work. (2)

2 He can escape. (2)

3 We can conquer. (2)

4 I was not able to/could not wait. (3)

5 They were able to/could flee. (2)

6 I cannot return. (3)

7 We could not run.* (3)

8 They were able to attack. (2)

9 I cannot sleep. (3)

10 You could not fight.* (3)

Total: 25

Exercise 16.5

1 The sailors were able to sail to the island.* (5)

2 We will never be able to conquer the enemy. (4)

3 The soldiers were not able to destroy the city.* (5)

4 The slaves were not able to escape from the town.* (6)

5 The soldiers will be able to capture this town. (5)

6 The Romans could not throw their missiles.* (5)

7 That king cannot rule well. (6)

8 The citizens were not able to defend the city well.* (6)

9 That slave cannot drink this wine. (7)

10 We were not able to come to the city today.* (6)

Total: 55

Exercise 16.6

1 Who will be able to come to the temple tomorrow? (6)

2 We will never be able to make this long journey. (6)

3 The soldiers cannot cross this river. (6)

4 The master was not able to set that slave free.* (6)

5 The comrades were not able to run quickly.* (5)

6 Teachers cannot do everything. (5)

7 The Greeks were not able to conquer the Romans in this battle.* (8)

8 This man will not be able to write a long book. (7)

9 I was not able to give much money to my son.* (7)

10 The tired soldiers were not able to fight well against these enemies.* (9)

Total: 65

*Note: The alternatives 'could/could not' and 'were/were not able' are permissible as appropriate.

Exercise 16.7

1 legere possum. (2)

2 effugere non poteramus/potuimus. (3)

3 ridere non potes. (3)

4 laborare non potero. (3)

5 oppugnare non poterant/potuerunt. (3)

6 navigare possum. (2)

7 cantare poterat/potuit. (2)

8 venire poterunt. (2)

9 videre non poterant/potuerunt. (3)

10 discedere potestis. (2)

Total: 25

Exercise 16.8

1 hic puer vinum bibere non potest.

2 cives oppidum defendere non poterunt.

3 discipuli hoc facere non potuerunt.

4 hostes pecuniam civium invenire non poterant/potuerunt.

5 dux copias maximas parare non poterat/potuit.

5 marks for each question. Total: 25

Exercise 16.9

1 mox ex urbibus effugiemus.   We will soon escape from the cities.   (3 + 4)

2 reges nobiles sunt.   The kings are noble.   (3 + 3)

3 urbes defendemus.   We will defend the cities.   (2 + 2)

4 puellas videratis.   You had seen the girls.   (2 + 2)

5 amicos exspectabant.   They were waiting for friends.   (2 + 2)

Total: 25

Exercise 16.10

1 servus currit.   The slave is running.

2 amicus effugiebat.   The friend was escaping.

3 hostem invenisti.   You found the enemy.

4 militem servaveram.   I had saved the soldier.

5 telum habebam.   I had a missile.

2 + 2 marks for each question. Total: 20

Exercise 16.11

1 eunt.   They go.   (1 + 1)

2 oppida numquam aedificavimus.   We never built towns.   (2 + 3)

3 pueri puellas amabant.   The boys loved the girls.   (3 + 3)

4 duces milites fessos defendebant.   The generals were defending the tired soldiers. (2 + 3)

5 fortiter pugnabimus.   We will fight bravely.   (2 + 2)

Total: 25

Exercise 16.12

1 redii.   I returned/have returned.   (1 + 1)

2 ille civis effugiebat.   That citizen was escaping.   (3 + 3)

3 murus ingens erat.   The wall was huge.   (3 + 3)

4 discipulus bene laboravit.   The pupil worked well.   (2 + 3)

5 mulier templum spectabat.   The woman was looking at the temple.   (3 + 3)

Total: 25

Exercise 16.13

1 potest.   He can.

2 servabitis.   You will save.

3 invenerunt.   They found.

4 iimus/ivimus.   We went.

5 vincebas.   You were conquering.

2 marks for each question. Total: 10

Exercise 16.14

1 He was able.	3rd person	Singular	possum
2 We were hurrying.	1st person	Plural	festino
3 They will escape.	3rd person	Plural	effugio
4 We were.	1st person	Plural	sum
5 He was perishing.	3rd person	Singular	pereo

4 marks for each question. Total: 20

Exercise 16.15

1 vulnus illud crudele erat. (4)

2 tela hostium timemus. (3)

3 urbem nostram telis oppugnaverunt. (4)

4 hostes nobiles erant. (3)

5 iter non longum sed difficile est. (6)

Total: 20

Exercise 16.16

1 rex ex urbe effugit.

2 hostes minimam insulam oppugnaverunt.

3 Romani bene pugnare poterant.

4 nautae ad insulam navigaverunt.

5 virtute militum oppidum cepimus.

4 marks for each question. Total: 20

Exercise 17.1

The Greeks had built a very big wooden horse.[5] Before they departed in their ships,[4] they put very many soldiers in the horse[5] and abandoned the horse on the shore near the city.[7]

When the Trojans saw the horse,[4] they went out of the gates.[2] They were amazed.[2] They were looking at the horse for a long time.[3] One of the Trojans said these words:[5] 'The Greeks have departed.[2] We have conquered them, haven't we?[3] This horse is a gift for us.[5] You must pull it into the middle of the city, citizens!'[7]

A second Trojan however shouted in a loud voice:[6] 'This horse is not a gift for us, is it?[6] Greeks never give gifts.[4] Greeks are deceitful people.[4] Don't pull the horse into the city, citizens![6] We must destroy it!'[3]

Finally the Trojans decided to pull the horse into the city.[7]

Total: 90

Exercise 17.2

1 (a) aedificaverant.   (1)

  (b) in/prope/e.   (1)

  (c) secundus.   (1)

  (d) nolite.   (1)

2 equum means 'horse' and equestrian describes something concerning horses.   (1)

3 Ablative. After the preposition in.   (2)

4 pono.   (1)

5 Subject: **Troiani.**   Object: **equum.**   (2)

Total: 10

Exercise 17.3

1 Don't laugh, boy!   6 Don't go in, young man!

2 Don't laugh, boys!   7 Don't sail, sailors!

3 Don't attack, soldiers!   8 Don't stand, father!

4 Don't escape, slaves!   9 Don't play, girls!

5 Don't wait, friend!   10 Don't depart, mother!

3 marks for each question. Total: 30

1 Don't cry, woman! (3)

2 Don't write books, poets! (4)

3 Don't run, soldier! (3)

4 Don't sit, girl! (3)

5 Don't be afraid, comrades! (3)

6 Don't stay here, citizens! (4)

7 Don't fight, bad boys! (4)

8 Don't hurry, slave! (3)

9 Don't sing, daughters! (3)

10 Don't leave me here, friends! (5)

Total: 35

Exercise 17.5

1 Don't attack the town, soldiers! (4)

2 Don't listen to the teacher's words, boys! (5)

3 Don't make the long journey, friend! (5)

4 Don't defend the city against the enemy, citizens! (6)

5 Don't punish this slave, master! (5)

6 Don't set free those slaves, masters! (5)

7 Don't go out of the temple, boy! (5)

8 Don't hand over the money to your father, young man! (5)

9 Don't stand in the road, girls! (5)

10 Don't drink this wine, mother! (5)

Total: 50

Exercise 17.6

1 nolite currere, puellae!

2 noli appropinquare, puer!

3 nolite ruere, milites!

4 noli redire, amice!

5 nolite laborare, discipuli!

6 nolite pugnare, comites!

7 nolite oppugnare, servi!

8 noli festinare, mater!

9 nolite respondere, pueri!

10 nolite pugnare, cives!

3 marks for each question. Total: 30

Exercise 17.7

1 noli in via ludere, puer! (5)

2 nolite hostes vulnerare, milites! (4)

3 noli hunc servum liberare, domine! (5)

4 noli flumen transire, nauta! (4)

5 nolite illum magistrum audire, discipuli! (5)

6 noli pecuniam tradere, rex! (4)

7 nolite urbem oppugnare, Romani! (4)

8 nolite hastas iacere, servi! (5)

9 noli regem necare/occidere, serve! (4)

10 noli omne vinum bibere, puella! (5)

Total: 45

Exercise 17.8

1 He is crying. (1)

2 He isn't crying, is he? (2)

3 He's crying, isn't he? (2)

4 They are fighting. (1)

5 Are they fighting? (1)

6 They aren't fighting, are they? (2)

7 They have escaped. (1)

8 Have they escaped? (1)

9 They have escaped, haven't they? (2)

10 They haven't escaped, have they? (2)

Total: 15

Exercise 17.9

1 He was fighting well. (2)

2 He was fighting well, wasn't he? (3)

3 He wasn't fighting well, was he? (3)

4 This soldier is brave. (4)

5 This soldier is brave, isn't he? (5)

6 This soldier is not brave, is he? (5)

7 Hector was a bold soldier. (4)

8 Hector was a bold soldier, wasn't he? (4)

9 Hector was not a bold soldier, was he? (5)

10 Hector was not the bravest of the Trojans, was he? (5)

Total: 40

Exercise 17.10

1 The citizens were defending the city well, weren't they? (5)

2 The boy didn't do this, did he? (4)

3 The Greeks didn't conquer the Romans, did they? (4)

4 Not everyone is afraid of death, are they? (4)

5 You caught sight of that girl in the city yesterday, didn't you? (7)

6 You do love your mother, don't you? (4)

7 The Greeks collected many weapons, didn't they? (5)

8 The woman won't be able to do this, will she? (5)

9 The Roman soldiers fought well in the war, didn't they? (7)

10 It isn't difficult to do this, is it? (5)

Total: 50

Exercise 17.11

1 nonne Romani sumus? (3)

2 num Romani sumus? (3)

3 Romanine sumus? (2)

4 num curris? (2)

5 currisne? (1)

6 nonne curris? (2)

7 num ridebas? (2)

8 nonne ridebas? (2)

9 ridebasne? (1)

10 num effugiemus? (2)

Total: 20

Exercise 17.12

1 num hic vir sapientissimus est?

2 nonne haec arma bona sunt?

3 num iter illud facile est?

4 nonne illam puellam miseram vidisti?

5 nonne hanc urbem cras oppugnabimus?

5 marks for each questions. Total: 25

Exercise 17.13

1 num vir uxorem suam amat?

2 nonne Romani hostes superabunt/vincent?

3 num hoc facere poterimus?

4 nonne ille miles vulnus accepit?

5 nonne mors ad omnes veniet?

4 marks for each question. Total: 20

Exercise 17.14

1 clamamus.	We shout.	(1 + 1)
2 reginae adveniebant.	The queens were arriving.	(2 + 2)
3 puellas heri conspeximus.	We caught sight of the girls yesterday.	(2 + 3)
4 mulieres optimas cenas parabant.	The women were preparing very good dinners.	(4 + 4)
5 duces amicos reliquerunt.	The generals abandoned their friends.	(3 + 3)

Total: 25

Exercise 17.15

1 colligebam.	I was collecting.	(1 + 1)
2 vocem semper audit.	He always hears a voice.	(2 + 3)
3 miles bene pugnavit.	The soldier fought well.	(2 + 3)
4 discipulus comitem non habebat.	The pupil did not have a comrade.	(3 + 4)
5 civis ducem audiebat.	The citizen was listening to the general.	(3 + 3)

Total: 25

Exercise 17.16

1 filia mea vocem bonam habet. (5)

2 vir sapiens est. (3)

3 multi viri sapientes non sunt. (5)

4 Romani cras oppugnabunt. (3)

5 noli/nolite pecuniam ibi relinquere! (4)

Total: 20

Exercise 17.17

1 voces illarum puellarum audimus. (4)

2 pueri in media via stant. (5)

3 multam pecuniam in via reliquit. (5)

4 cives arma in urbe reliquerunt. (5)

5 omnes milites Romani magnam virtutem habebant. (6)

Total: 25

Exercise 17.18

1 We have conquered the enemy. (2)

2 He has written a book. (2)

3 They have found much money. (3)

4 The slaves escaped. (2)

5 They threw missiles. (2)

6 The poet will come tomorrow. (3)

7 He received a wound. (2)

8 My father has departed. (3)

9 They went out of the city. (3)

10 He said that word. (3)

Total: 25

Exercise 18.1

The Trojans dragged the horse into the city.[5] They were very happy because the Greeks had departed.[5] They were very happy because they had conquered the Greeks.[5]

Therefore that night all the citizens were holding a celebration.[6] They were eating much food and drinking much wine.[7] Soon all the Trojans were sleeping.[4]

In the middle of the night the Greek soldiers[4] who were in the horse[4] climbed down from the horse in silence.[4] Suddenly they charged at the Trojans as they were sleeping, with loud shouts.[6] The Trojans were not able to defend themselves.[5] Many Trojans perished by the swords of the Greeks.[5] Among these was the old man Priam, king of Troy.[7] The Greeks left few Trojans alive.[5]

In this way the Greeks captured the city of Troy by trickery after ten years.[8] They destroyed the greatest part of the city.[4] They were now able to lead Helen back to Greece.[6]

Total: 90

Exercise 18.2

1 (a) laetissimi/maximam. (1)

   (b) erant/celebrabant/consumebant/bibebant/dormiebant/
     poterant/erat. (1)

   (c) in/ad/inter/post. (1)

   (d) defendere/reducere. (1)

2 3rd person   Plural   Pluperfect   vinco (4)

3 Accusative. Object of the verb. (2)

Total: 10

Exercise 18.3

1 That boy loves himself. (4)

2 The Romans decided to kill themselves. (4)

3 The Trojans prepared to defend themselves. (4)

4 That girl is always looking at herself. (5)

5 The general ordered the soldiers to make the journey with him. (6)

6 Wise pupils never praise themselves. (5)

7 The Trojan citizens were defending themselves bravely. (5)

8 That soldier wounded himself with his own sword. (6)

9 The sad citizens handed themselves over to the enemy. (5)

10 Many women were looking at themselves in the river. (6)

Total: 50

Exercise 18.4

1 This old man isn't dead, is he? (5)

2 Many perished, few escaped. (4)

3 Don't abandon me, comrades! (4)

4 We heard the shouts of many old men. (5)

5 These brave soldiers want to save themselves. (6)

6 Fight well, citizens! (3)

7 The Greeks are not braver than us. (6)

8 The Greek soldiers were very lucky, weren't they? (5)

9 You are safe, we are in great danger. (8)

10 Who will be able to save us? (4)

Total: 50

Exercise 18.5

1 The old man was both brave and bold. (6)

2 That boy is not standing in the middle of the road, is he? (7)

3 Not all the citizens were brave. (5)

4 That general will never be able to capture this town. (7)

5 The enemy were not able to cross the river. (5)

6 Soldiers always like a lucky general. (5)

7 My father has a loud voice. (5)

8 When the Greeks captured Troy, they led Helen back to Greece. (8)

9 The Trojans were defending their city well, weren't they? (6)

10 The shouts of those frightened women were loud. (6)

Total: 60

Exercise 18.6

1 When the gods and goddesses saw the goddess Discord, they were very angry. (9)

2 When Paris took Helen, Menelaus sent messengers to all his comrades. (10)

3 When the Greeks heard about Helen, they sent forces to Menelaus. (9)

4 When the forces of the Greeks sailed across the sea, they attacked Troy. (8)

5 When Achilles killed Hector, he was happy. (6)

6 When the Greeks built a big horse, they left it near the city. (9)

7 When the Greeks left the horse near the city, they departed. (7)

8 When the Trojans saw the horse, they were afraid. (5)

9 When many Trojans saw Greeks in the middle of the city, they fled. (9)

10 When the Greeks destroyed the city of Troy, they returned to Greece. (8)

Total: 80

Exercise 18.7

1 Although this man is a sailor, he is afraid of water. (7)

2 Although Achilles was a bold soldier, he did not want to fight. (8)

3 Although the Greeks attacked Troy for a long time, they were not able to capture the city with their weapons. (10)

4 Although the Greeks were better soldiers than the Trojans, they did not fight well. (10)

5 Although I am wiser than many people, I do not have much money. (10)

6 Although the Trojans defended the city well, they were not able to save it. (9)

7 Although the soldier was tired, he fought for a long time. (6)

8 Although the teacher was very wise, the pupils did not like him. (8)

9 Although the old man's voice was loud, we were not able to hear it. (9)

10 Although the citizens were afraid of the enemy, they fought well against them. (8)

Total: 85

Exercise 18.8

1 auditis. You hear. (1 + 1)

2 senes non timebant. The old men were not afraid. (2 + 3)

3 tela longa erant. The missiles were long. (3 + 3)

4 agricolae equos habent. The farmers have horses. (3 + 3)

5 iuvenes hastas tenebant. The young men were holding spears. (3 + 3)

Total: 25

Exercise 18.9

1 possum. I am able. (1 + 1)

2 puellam reduxit. He led the girl back. (2 + 2)

3 clamorem hominis audivi. I heard a man's shout. (3 + 3)

4 discipulus non respondit.   The pupil did not reply.   (2 + 3)

5 miles proelium non saepe timebat.   The soldier was not often afraid of the battle. (3 + 5)

Total: 25

Exercise 18.10

1 reducemus.   We will lead back.

2 relinquebant.   They were leaving.

3 poterat.   He was able.

4 conspexi.   I caught sight of.

5 bibitis.   You drink.

2 marks for each question. Total: 10

Exercise 18.11

1 He put.	3rd person	Singular	Perfect	pono
2 He was able.	3rd person	Singular	Perfect	possum
3 They led back.	3rd person	Plural	Perfect	reduco
4 You escaped.	2nd person	Singular	Perfect	effugio
5 We will leave.	1st person	Plural	Future	relinquo

5 marks for each question. Total: 25

Exercise 18.12

1 nonne multi cives vivi erant?   (4)

2 paucae feminae/mulieres in urbe manebant.   (5)

3 nolite timere, amici! hoc facere potero.   (6)

4 senes sunt sapientiores quam iuvenes.   (5)

5 (nos) servi dominos crudelissimos omnes habemus.   (5)

Total: 25

Exercise 18.13

1 et viri et feminae/mulieres magnas voces habent.   (7)

2 ille miles audacior quam hic est.   (6)

3 num Achilles miles fortissimus Graecorum erat?   (6)

4 Troiani equum in media urbe posuerunt.   (6)

5 viri sapientes opera difficilia saepe amant.   (5)

Total: 30

Exercise 18.14

1	servabat.	He was saving.
2	videbant.	They were seeing.
3	superabam.	I was overcoming.
4	aedificabamus.	We were building.
5	stabant.	They were standing.
6	timebant.	They were afraid.
7	delebatis.	You were destroying.
8	spectabat.	He was watching.
9	respondebant.	They were replying.
10	amabat.	He was loving.

2 marks for each question. Total: 20

Test exercises

Test 1

1 Acrisius was a famous king.(3) He used to rule the city of Argos.(3) He had one daughter.(3) The name of the daughter was Danae.(4) One day the gods announced to Acrisius:(4) 'Beware, Acrisius!(1) Your daughter will have a son.(4) This son will kill you.'(4) These words frightened Acrisius.(4) (30)

2 (a) sum. (1)

(b) 3rd person. (1)

(c) Dative. (1)

(d) Plural. (1)

3 (a) filiam claram habebam. (3)

(b) verba filium terrent. (3)

Total: 40

Test 2

1 Acrisius was afraid of the words of the gods.(3) He therefore decided to build a big tower.(5) When he did this, he put his daughter, named Danae, in the tower.(8) Then he ordered slaves to guard Danae.(5) 'In this way I will be safe,' said Acrisius.(5) However, he was not safe.(4) (30)

2 (a) Neuter. (1)

(b) Genitive. (1)

(c) facio. (1)

(d) aedificare/custodire. (1)

3 (a) filia deum timebat. (3)

(b) deus servos terret. (3)

Total: 40

Test 3

1 Jupiter was king of the gods.(4) Although Juno, the queen of the gods, was his wife,(7) he often used to love many other women.(5) After he saw the beautiful Danae,(4) he decided to love her also.(4) He therefore entered the tower(3) and loved Danae.(3) (30)

2 (a) sum. (1)

(b) Accusative. (1)

(c) in. (1)

(d) 3rd person. (1)

3 (a) femina reginam amabat. (3)

(b) regina deum videt. (3)

Total: 40

Test 4

1 Afterwards, Danae gave birth to a little son.[4] The name of the boy was Perseus.[4] When Acrisius saw Perseus, he was frightened and angry.[8] He shouted: 'Who is the boy's father?'[5] Danae replied:[1] 'The boy's father is Jupiter, king of the gods.'[6] Acrisius decided to punish both the mother and her son.[7] (35)

2 (a) Genitive. (1)

(b) sum. (1)

(c) punire. (1)

(d) Feminine. (1)

3 (a) pueri parvi timent. (3)

(b) filius iratus clamabat. (3)

Total: 45

Test 5

1 Acrisius shut Danae and Perseus in a big chest.[8] Then he ordered slaves to carry the chest to the shore and throw it into the sea.[11] Danae and Perseus were frightened.[5] They were afraid of the waves.[2] Finally the waves drove the chest to an island.[6] There an old man named Dictys found and saved them.[8] (40)

2 (a) et. (1)

(b) iubeo. (1)

(c) Plural. (1)

(d) Ablative. (1)

3 (a) servus undas timebat. (3)

(b) insulam magnam amo. (3)

Total: 50

Test 6

1 Danae and Perseus lived happily on the island for a long time.[6] Perseus was now a young man[3] and his mother was still a beautiful woman.[7] When the king of the island, named Polydectes, caught sight of Danae,[7] he immediately loved her and wanted to marry her.[6] Perseus however did not like Polydectes.[5] He shouted to him:[2] 'You will never marry my mother.'[4] (40)

95

2 (a) diu/iam/adhuc/statim/tamen/numquam. (1)

(b) Imperfect. (1)

(c) Singular. (1)

(d) conspicio. (1)

3 (a) femina insulam amabat. (3)

(b) feminae bonae clamabant. (3)

Total: 50

Test 7

1 Perseus did not like Polydectes.(4) Polydectes did not like Perseus.(4) Perseus was brave but a young man.(5) He therefore said to the king: 'Polydectes,(5) I am not afraid of you.(4) I am a brave man.'(4) 'If you are a brave man,' replied Polydectes,(6) 'kill Medusa,(2) then bring her head to me!'(6) (40)

2 (a) sum. (1)

(b) Dative. (1)

(c) 1st person. (1)

(d) ego/te/eius/me. (1)

3 (a) Perseus Medusam necat. (3)

(b) puer puellam timebat. (3)

Total: 50

Test 8

1 These words of Polydectes frightened Perseus.(5) Although he was a brave young man, he was afraid of Medusa.(7) The gods and goddesses however gave help to Perseus.(7) They gave him a new sword and a polished shield.(7) When Perseus received these weapons, he was now happy.(7) He was not now afraid of Medusa.(4) He sailed from the island and travelled to Medusa.(8) (45)

2 (a) is. (1)

(b) do. (1)

(c) Ablative. After the preposition ab. (2)

3 (a) pueri gladios novos habent. (4)

(b) deam terremus. (2)

Total: 55

Test 9

1 The journey was long.(3) However after many dangers Perseus finally arrived at the land where Medusa lived.(13) He fought bravely with Medusa(4) and with the help of the gods killed her.(5) When he did this,(3) he cut off her head and returned to the island.(7)   (35)

2 (a) Neuter.   (1)

  (b) Accusative.   (1)

  (c) tamen/tandem/fortiter.   (1)

  (d) facio.   (1)

3 (a) pericula non timent.   (3)

  (b) deus insulam amabat.   (3)

Total: 45

Test 10

1 Perseus had killed Medusa.(2) He was now returning to Greece(4) and was carrying Medusa's head in a bag.(6) On the journey he caught sight of a beautiful girl.(5) The name of this girl was Andromeda.(4) She was frightened because a monster was attacking her.(6) Perseus however saved her.(4) He showed Medusa's head to the monster(4) and changed it into stone.(5)   (40)

2 (a) Pluperfect.   (1)

  (b) ad/in.   (1)

  (c) Genitive.   (1)

  (d) conspicio.   (1)

3 (a) Perseus Medusam videt.   (3)

  (b) puellam perterritam portabamus.   (3)

Total: 50

Test 11

1 When Perseus saved Andromeda,(4) he returned to Greece.(3) When Polydectes saw Perseus, he was angry.(6) 'What are you doing here?'(3) he shouted to Perseus.(2) 'You don't have Medusa's head, do you?'(5) Perseus replied:(2) 'I have killed Medusa and(3) I have her head here.(4) Look!'(1) Perseus showed Medusa's head.(4) Polydectes looked at the head(3) and was immediately changed into a rock.(5)   (45)

2 (a) Accusative.   (1)

  (b) redeo.   (1)

  (c) 2nd person.   (1)

  (d) hic/statim.   (1)

3 (a) Andromeda insulas videt. (3)

(b) Perseus Medusam spectabat. (3)

Total: 55

Test 12

1 Perseus had killed Polydectes.[3] Danae, the beautiful mother of Perseus, was now safe.[7] For a long time Perseus and Danae lived very happily.[6] One day Perseus travelled to the city of Larissa.[7] There athletics contests were being held.[2] Perseus threw a discus.[3] By chance the discus struck and killed a spectator.[6] This spectator was Acrisius.[4] The gods had spoken the truth.[3] Perseus had killed his own grandfather.[4]   (45)

2 (a) Accusative. (1)

(b) iacio. (1)

(c) Singular. (1)

(d) laetissimi. (1)

3 (a) Perseus avum necat. (3)

(b) dei laeti spectabant. (3)

Total: 55